Everything you want to know about Organisational Change

To Atul
Best Wishes!

Darren

Brian

Everything you want to know about Organisational Change

DARREN ARCANGEL AND
BRIAN JOHNSON

IT Governance Publishing

IT Governance Publishing
IT Governance Limited
Unit 3, Clive Court
Bartholomew's Walk
Cambridgeshire Business Park
Ely
Cambridgeshire
CB7 4EH
United Kingdom

www.itgovernance.co.uk

First published in the United Kingdom in 2011
by IT Governance Publishing.

ISBN 978-1-84928-197-3

FOREWORD

In every leadership position I've held, my philosophy has been the same: hire smart, self-motivated, creative people, and establish an environment conducive to teaming and leadership. I've found that to be particularly important in my current position as General Manager, Services, Support and Education for CA Technologies. One of the talents I admire most is the ability to create thought leadership, whether through an article, white paper or, in this case, a book.

The authoring of this book was the culmination of a multinational team effort. US-based authors, Brian and Darren, drew from the expertise and experience of a number of CA Services individuals. Most notable was Julie Tilke, VP Practice Services for Europe, from England. She was also an instrumental part of this work coming together.

The book is about organisations, and the complexities and dynamics that are found within them. It evaluates 'old school' and modern-day practices, and discusses the advantages of bringing the best of both 'worlds' together. In the book, Brian and Darren highlight a number of solid 'old school' practices that have largely been overlooked in recent times and discuss the value of modernisation of those practices.

It is also a book about people, the heart of all organisations, and how they are affected by technology. It explores how understanding the impact of technology on people can greatly improve the adoption of technology and the value that it brings.

Foreword

I hope you will enjoy this book and find it as thought provoking as I have.

Adam Elster
GM, Services Support and Education
CA Technologies

PREFACE

Why do organisations exist? This philosophical point is discussed in Chapter 1, though fundamentally the answer is that they fill a niche (or perhaps a better description is a need) in society.

Why do organisations change? This can probably be summed up in one of two ways: because people change their minds, and because everyone likes to be seen to be flexible (or agile, if current buzzword terminology is used).

One of the key attributes of the 'IT of the future' should be flexibility. In simple terms, this means that it should be possible for your portfolio of IT applications software to be changed quickly, and at minimum cost, whenever your business needs for IT support change. You can certainly count on the business needing faster access to greater quantities of information than ever before, from a growing spread of geographical locations; though it is impossible to predict what the information will be.

You will, unfortunately, also be faced with changes in technology, at least some of which will be intended to provide the very flexibility we are discussing. Flexibility is the main benefit of technology – not the much claimed cost-savings which many authorities dispute. Flexibility, including access to information wherever it may be stored, from any location, is the major benefit of the Internet and the World Wide Web. What is unfortunate, is that in many cases you will have to change your applications to allow them to run on the improved technology.

So there it is then, IT is the driver for business change and everything you do will be dependent on IT. Well, not so fast. IT outsourcing is more popular than ever, and the business world sees IT as the tail on the dog – not vice versa.

A reviewer of this book made the excellent suggestion that a statement should be made that IT change inevitably should follow business change. The ubiquity of IT tends to the belief that IT is the driver, the enabler and the goal of all change, whereas, in reality, it is no more than a tool for business. Despite all of our technological advances, people remain essential and people drive business.

IT may cause change to the business (and, therefore, to how the business organisation must change to accommodate new concepts, lines of business and consumption of IT), but that does not mean IT shapes the business organisation, or its hierarchies, or that it is anything more than a factor in understanding the job performed by a person.

By itself, IT is irrelevant in terms of hardware. Services provided by IT to support government, banking, insurance and so on, are based on applications developed to automate or support business processes. And most often, business change is driven by the need to change services, create new services, or simply to fix problems with existing services – in other words, applications development.

Deciding your requirements for new applications on the basis of a defined business need is by no means straightforward. It isn't like building a garage or a patio, where the end product is tangible, the planning, architectural and building work are well understood and straightforward, and the scope for changing your mind before, or after completion, is limited.

IT is complex, intangible, quite hard to understand, very easy to change, and hard to keep under control. The 'easy to change' statement perhaps needs a little more amplification. IT spends vast sums of money because it is complex and because it needs to control many thousands of changes every month. And yet, that very complexity is one of the reasons cited by IT for needing experts to manage change – because it is so difficult and so complex, it needs expensive monitoring software to keep things under control, and many highly-paid experts to ensure change goes well.

These experts tell you how hard it is to change IT – what they really mean is how hard it is to change IT successfully – without detriment, or the need for further change, or indeed, the need to back out of ill-conceived changes.

The truth is that IT is far too easy to change, and the IT organisation is often predicated on managing change, instead of managing the delivery of more reliable services.

It is not easy for business and IT people to talk about the IT requirements of the business because it is claimed that IT requires precise language. The plain words spoken by business are clearly imprecise then …

Of course, the root problem is that IT wants business to communicate in quasi-technical language and the business is paying IT to support business. What should bring both sides together is a properly planned programme of change, where requirements are fully understood, specifications agreed by both sides, organisational impact assessed and risks are identified and managed.

In short, this is the time for detailed project planning and project execution within the framework of the change programme. Some IT preparation may be possible in advance of the change, but much of it will have to be done during the change. You may need projects to manage some, or all, of the following IT-related changes.

Infrastructure acquisition

- Acquire application package software
- Develop bespoke software
- Acquire underpinning IT infrastructure (system software, telecommunications facilities).

Infrastructure integration

- Smoothly integrate new IT infrastructure with existing
- Infrastructure management
- Improve the management, or control, of the IT infrastructure.

Continuity of support

- Ensure existing IT facilities operate smoothly until replaced, or no longer required
- Ensure arrangements exist for fall-back and disaster recovery.

Business readiness

- Prepare business and IT users to cope with changes
- Accommodation changes
- Prepare the physical accommodation and environment for the changes.

Undertaking changes of this scale, so that everything happens in the right sequence and at the right time, is a matter of careful planning, good organisation and readiness to deal with the unforeseen.

And key to all of the issues associated with smoothly managing change, is understanding and managing how the organisation must change (not only in the business as new practices are rolled out, but also in IT, where new skills may be needed and where technology change has a major impact on the role of support staff).

And *then* there are the people issues ...

ABOUT THE AUTHORS

Darren Arcangel is a VP, Principal Services Architect at CA Technology. Since joining CA in early 2008, he has been the lead architect for some of CA Technology's largest enterprise IT service management implementations. These implementations involve the company's key business objectives, span multiple processes, and involve the integration of a variety of business and IT applications.

Prior to joining CA Technologies, Darren held several architect positions at HP, focusing on large-scale IT transformations. He was a SWAT team member of the HP's large-scale IT transformation programme. These transformations included programme/project governance; standardisation of applications and infrastructure; an enterprise data warehouse; SOA; data centre transformations and IT service management.

Darren holds a Master of Science degree from Boston University; is an ITIL® v3 expert in IT service management; and has been recognised as an ITAC Master Certified Architect from The Open Group.

Darren lives in Southern California and enjoys participating in numerous outdoor activities with his wife and three children.

Brian Johnson joined CA Technology Services in 2004, after leaving key leadership and strategic roles as the Director of Product Development in Pink Elephant. Prior to that he held a senior civil servant position where, as a board member of the Office of Government Commerce, he designed and led the Key Strategy on Knowledge Management.

At OGC he was (not surprisingly) Director of Knowledge Management and responsible for overall management of OGC marketing, service desk, Web and ePresence teams. Brian led the major project within OGC that created the first government service desk based on customer needs. Other senior civil service positions include management positions in operational services, senior systems design and capacity management.

Brian was part of the UK government team that created the ITIL® approach. Working for the Central Computer and Telecommunications Agency (now part of the Office of Government Commerce), Brian authored many of the first ITIL® books and designed both the ITIL® business perspective series and version two of ITIL®. His version one book *Software Lifecycle Support*, written with software testing guru, Richard Warden, covered the roles of the business, IT operations and development in designing IT services; one of the central tenets of the version three ITIL® books.

Brian has authored, or co-authored, more than 20 titles on ITIL®, project management and related subjects. He also prefers to play football to just about anything.

ACKNOWLEDGEMENTS

Adam Elster (General Manager, CA Technologies): For providing executive support and for his Foreword.

Tyson Faulkner and Ed Furilla (CA Technologies): For their excellent contributions, in particular the Appendix on acquisitions and mergers.

Dr John Stewart: He created the IT Infrastructure Library® (ITIL®) and is rarely credited for the achievement.

Rene van't Veen and Arnold van Mameren: Two Dutchmen who were, and are, significantly ahead of their time in the field of organisational change, and whose original work I was privileged to use in ITIL® Version one.

Julie Tilke and Peter Doherty (CA Technologies): For their diligent reviews and intelligent suggestions.

John, Rene and Arnold were 20 years ahead of their time, and some of their discarded gems have been reinvented in this book.

ir. H.L. (Maarten) Souw RE, IT-Auditor, UWV and Giuseppe G. Zorzino CISA CGEIT CRISC, Security Architect, Tecnoindex SpA who reviewed the draft manuscript and provided useful feedback.

All royalties are donated to Dogs Trust: *www.dogstrust.org.uk*.

ITIL® is a Registered Trade Mark of the Office of Government Commerce in the United Kingdom and other countries.

Acknowledgements

IT Infrastructure Library® is a Registered Trade Mark of the Office of Government Commerce in the United Kingdom and other countries.

CONTENTS

Contents

Contents

INTRODUCTION

Organisational change has been the subject of many books, and will continue to be the subject of many more. This book considers such change in the modern context of information systems and information technology, both being enablers (and sometimes inhibitors) of business change.

IT is often considered to be inextricably linked to business – mostly by IT pundits; however, the popularity of outsourcing IT, and the increasing profile of software being provided as a service, are proof points that business may not share that point of view. If IT does not deliver value and benefit, it will be outsourced, no argument.

The book, therefore, does not hold IT as an essential partner to business and it does not consider *only* IT in the role of organisational change. Instead, it considers first the human capital of change, and second, the role (or rather the potential role in many instances) that might be played by IT. Most often, IT can be a catalyst or agent for change, though it should be recognised that IT is not a magic bullet for shaping the human aspects of change.

CHAPTER 1: WHY DO ORGANISATIONS EXIST?

The fundamental question

A politically incorrect answer to this question would be that organisations exist to allow individuals to make money (in the private sector), or to wield power (in the public sector). After all, in the case of the former, the world economy is dependent on businesses making capital and creating wealth and, in the case of the latter, whether democratically elected, or simply being the ruling party, society would fail to function if it were not organised. Of course, the degree of satisfaction we have with either organisation entirely depends on where you sit.

If we examine the question from either the private or public perspective, it seems clear that if organisations did not exist, we would need to create them, because who/what else would address the following questions; what … ?

- Is the state of our economy?
- … and the world economies?
- Is the most important change taking place in our sector of the market?
- Are the demands of the environment?
- Is the impact on this business (or this government body)?
- Should we be planning for to ensure our long-term future?
- Products and services will be needed?
- Are our current capabilities?
- New technologies will help us?
- Are our strategic objectives?

- Specific actions must we take, and in what time-frame?
- Support will we need?
- Skills are present in our top management team and what others will we need?
- Kind of action plan can we agree on?
- Will be our communications strategy (internal and external)?
- Can we create as a roadmap or model, to provide a common picture of any change effort?
- Can we get each senior manager to define as criteria for success?
- Are the decisions to be made, or questions to be answered, at executive level?
- Specific sets of employees will be implementing change and, therefore, expected to understand the change?
- New skills will they need?
- Have we communicated to the executive and business levels about goals?

Why IT?

Why mention IT specifically? Largely because IT is now ubiquitous; it is almost inconceivable to imagine a business that is not dependent on IT in some form (even if it is simply an address on the Internet for a restaurant or public house perhaps, where potential customers can find information).

These days IT is not so much an enabler of change, but more of a catalyst. That does not mean IT is either 'integrated', or necessarily 'aligned' with the business of the business (in fact it is often perceived as being as remote, or insensitive, as it ever was). The issue is that some IT services/concepts have been taken on board by organisations in such a way that IT has become much more commoditised in some areas, and yet remains difficult to change at the fundamental level (by that we do not refer to the out-of-control, day-to-day change that is simply too easy to request and, indeed, out of control). The reference is to the change sometimes considered for fundamental services – which, in turn, comprise application building blocks and specific hardware – which is simply too expensive to contemplate unless major, material advantages will quickly accrue.

IT often does not know how to align to the business properly, and that leads to this misalignment; a statement which applies irrespective of the nature of the business – private sector, government or otherwise. This is not to say that people in IT do not try. It is quite common for IT to have senior staff members whose job it is to 'represent' different elements of the business. It is quite common to find, though, that these resources only have (at best) a tactical understanding of the business unit they represent. Most often they are recruited from within IT, and guess what? They have an IT view of the business.

They do not necessarily get involved with business strategy decisions or business planning sessions. Unfortunately, this lack of business understanding leads to a reactionary relation between IT and business. IT is instructed at the last minute that a new service or system must be built – or sometimes installed. Or worse, that the business has just purchased an expensive business software solution that IT must now support. In some cases, business buys a service and because of the nature of the Internet, is able to use the service – until something goes wrong, perhaps many months after purchase. At which time, IT is asked for support – often the first that anyone in IT even knew that a new IT system was in use!

IT needs to be involved with business planning and strategy sessions in order to truly align with the business. It is in this way that IT can be more useful. Some suggestions include:

- From the IT perspective; recommending solutions to automate business processes.
- And from the business side; providing IT management with early warnings about plans that will impact current skill sets, staffing or IT support/capacity needs.

For an organisation to exist without some strategic view of its second most expensive investment (people being the primary and most important spend) is tantamount to commercial suicide.

This is not to argue that IT changes or drives change to the organisation, it is a recognition that the business drive to reduce overheads through greater use of IT, will inevitably lead to organisational change. How to manage that change is not, however, necessarily in the gift of IT.

The business environment

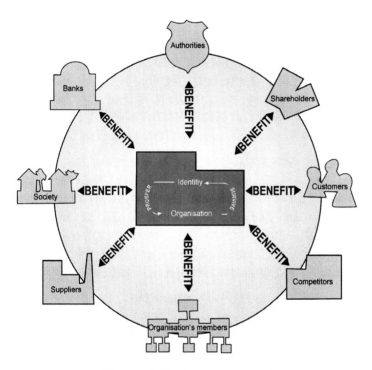

Figure 1: Business eco-systems

It is worthwhile spending some time considering the fundamental causes of change in business, and why some changes are easier to survive than others. Figure 1 illustrates some of the main business eco-systems. It illustrates what are institutionalised stakeholders; in each instance the organisation exists only to provide some form of benefit. Where the business is operating in a well-established sector, providing well-known products or services in a stable or niche market, it is likely that IT capabilities are well matched to business needs. Changes are unlikely to be dramatic and should be easy to manage and survive.

In such a situation, if the market begins to change, the synergy between the business and IT is probably reflected in the business and IS strategies for the future. In that case, IT will be an enabler of the changes and any business transformation. Although more risk is involved, survival is more a matter of good management and planning.

In situations where the business is operating in a stable market, and gaps are found between the business requirement for IT support, and the IT capabilities that are available to the business, fundamental change in IT is necessary. The ability to survive is, to an extent, dependent on the scale of the change and the speed with which it has to be undertaken, but once more the risks can be controlled.

If the capabilities of the IT organisation are not aligned with the business strategy, and the business capabilities of the business are not aligned with their market, then the business is presented with very significant challenges.

If IT is a significant stakeholder in change, should not then the business take a view on the capabilities in IT? Figure 2 provides a viewpoint for the business. Strictly speaking, the prevalent competence of your IT sets the stage for its deployment (what is possible); and the deployment is partially responsible for the business results.

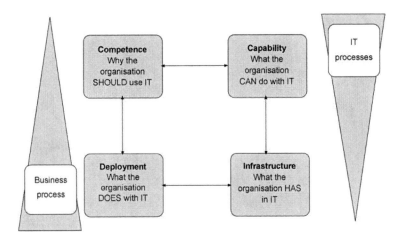

Figure 2: How IT should be viewed by business

A required competence requires a set of IT capabilities, which, in turn, enable the organisation to use its IT effectively. The hardware and software used by IT is the infrastructure, and is (or should be) an invisible, but important, asset for the business, but one wholly managed by the trusted service provider. Changing the infrastructure of course means new capabilities, new competence requirements and, of course, should result in better deployment of IT.

The loop is one of continual feedback, with the elements necessarily influencing the other.

The deployment element, of course, creates demand upon the infrastructure and, in turn, the infrastructure is necessary to support deployment.

The business must be aware that change predicated on using IT will have implications across each element. This is further covered in Chapter 6. The key element of change then is its widespread effect.

For example:

- Decisions that you, and other managers, make in the business, are affected, e.g. where you would take one position on an investment in the past, you would now take a different position because of economic fluctuations.
- Usefulness of IT deployed in the business area in economic terms is enhanced (or reduced), since the methods to determine the degree of support, or perhaps the lack of it, have changed.
- The IT services used in the business area gradually change as the IT infrastructure changes (maybe because the business starts to procure IT services from outside, because it is seen to be more responsive than internal IT).

Organisations exist to provide benefit to a variety of putative stakeholders. Shareholders receive benefit from their investment in private sector companies, for example. Governments provide benefit to their citizens (though that might be a debatable point depending on where you live). Banks were initially created for purposes not entirely linked to getting rich at the expense of their customers, and many of the benefits are consequent on an eco-system of different organisations. All of these types of benefit are (or should be) the focus of the organisation created to provide them.

How the organisations are structured and managed is, however, unique, even in the same vertical sector. For example, government is government, but does anyone really believe that the French govern in the same way as the English? Or that politics in the US is not influenced by the media more than in any other country? Or that all countries have a free press?

The same is true of other organisations working in the same vertical, whether oil, pharmaceutical or IT; characteristics may be similar, but ways of working, management and pretty much everything else, may be labelled the same way, yet do not exist in the same way.

What is the function of the organisation?

As mentioned earlier, a cynical answer would be to ensure that it continues to exist, and sometimes cynicism is reality. If businesses are to flourish, an organisation and a hierarchy must exist. Even very small organisations exist primarily to serve themselves; a shopkeeper may have only one employee, but that employee exists to help maintain the business of that shop – the hierarchy is flat, but, nevertheless, it exists. And furthermore, the bullet list of questions that we began with at the beginning of the chapter, will be applicable, albeit at a level of effort commensurate with the scale of the business.

A new till may be a future purchase, for example, for a small corner shop business. Maybe the owner should buy a BlackBerry? Or in a large organisation, many BlackBerries, if the business wishes to improve communications. Or, maybe a shared workspace should be built/acquired to cut down on e-mailing ... The point we are making is that boundaries often exist that are not bridged by one domain of expertise.

The crucial point is that all organisations are predicated on the Darwinian concept of 'survival of the fittest', even if they teach Creationism.

Corporate culture

So how do we get people to think across boundaries? Why is it important for organisations to work across boundaries? Is it speed and execution perhaps? We will elaborate on these issues throughout this book. We should also point out that elaboration is not the same as guidance. By and large, most organisations will face similar challenges, so we have created checklists that we believe all organisations will be able to use to orient their decision-making processes. But the question of guidance is another issue. Every organisation will have a different corporate culture and goals, and so it is impossible (and pretty stupid) to pretend that we – or come to that anyone else – has the single golden nugget that will change for the better everything that is, or should be, done. How you answer the questions in the context of your own organisation, is the most important factor; where possible, we provide some ideas and some examples that may assist, though, as we will often reiterate, there is no one, universal answer.

An example of perpetuating the organisation

Is there then one sure-fire way to help the organisation survive? Let's take a look at a good example of how one organisation manages changes.

To facilitate change and improved business processes, the US Department of Defense provides official, documented guidance about authorised methods. One approach is corporate information management, which has a specific directive concerning change through automation. The directive suggests that you should think first about the best way to perform an important action, and then automate only the necessary information: avoid automating ineffective or unnecessary processes.

The US Department of Defense checklist for change includes:

- Adopt a business engineering approach to business management
- Focus on the mission of the business
- Identify the business activity to be evaluated
- Define the goals
- Create a strategy to achieve goals
- Identify options (through in-depth analysis of data requirements and business processes)
- Perform risk analysis
- Assess costs for the options
- Perform cost-benefit analysis to help decision making
- Create management teams for the programme of change
- Create plans for implementation
- Streamline, simplify, or consolidate added value activities
- Eliminate ineffective activities
- Improve business processes
- Take opportunities offered by IT to automate the improved processes
- Review progress regularly.

Fairly innocuous stuff really, and hard to argue with. One can see parallels with lots of published good practice. Unless your goals are not 'Defense (spelled the American way) of the Nation … '

A contrary view of this would be:

'Nothing really changes does it? Those in power, stay in power. No vision, only procedures. Plenty of opportunity for red tape, scapegoating, etc. This stuff is more inclined to stifle change, rather than facilitate it. However, the list does illustrate "things that should be done". But the most interesting thing is that even though the role and importance of the military might have changed since the fall of the Eastern bloc, it obviously has not changed their unduly rigorous views about handling change. No room for adaptation, no room for innovation. No room for anything except step-by-step precision.

Everyone is different and every change is different, so think about issues before you do anything. The Department of Defense goals of most likely, defending the nation*, do not bear any relation to goals of surviving transitions, prosperity, growth … Because their goals are based on their own, perceived, socio-economic importance – which has not changed even though the world has, and the world view of the socio-economic importance of the military is completely different.'

Less contentious description of 'Killing people more effectively'.

This book is not intended to provide specific answers to creation, or change to organisations, precisely because of the diversity of organisation types (and people running them), as this short example illustrates. It is, however, intended to discuss the issues facing all organisations, and to describe the methods that can be used to address some of those issues. The most important advice in here is that there is no silver bullet – no matter what someone tries to sell you.

In the next chapter, we will discuss some of the reasons why organisations change – some more frequently than others.

CHAPTER 2: WHY CHANGE THE ORGANISATION?

Change is inevitable

Change is nothing new in business. It is an inevitable consequence of existence – as Sartre certainly did not say, but that is, however, a certainty in itself. Most businesses are accustomed to continual change. What is new, is the scale of change affecting business. It has become commonplace for business to experience radical, dramatic, far-reaching and fundamental change. So much so, that what is regarded as life-changing, is now largely a matter of perception. To some, a new line of business, or the outsourcing of non-core activities, might be a dramatic change; to others, such changes may be viewed as routine.

Less than amusing to most people is the scale of change in IT; either IT is incredibly messed up because it was engineered by a five-year-old (or a whole posse of five-year-olds), or the basic building blocks were just thrown together because no one really knew anything other than how wires should be joined together.

The latter is most likely.

IT is in constant change it seems, from minutiae (self-inflicted damage) to major, life-changing failures that inevitably lead to press headlines about the latest waste of money on purpose-built, complex projects. Ironically, one of the causes is the way organisations have evolved to eliminate time-consuming irritations, such as having to communicate plans. Such communications generally led to hearing things that were unpopular.

Prior to engaging in major consultations to transform, some simple considerations can be identified, that most, if not all, organisations will have at least discussed in past times.

Some of the considerations will be:

- The need to engage with business leaders and mindshare, in order to affect any organisational change.
- The business requiring the change may need to consider tradeoffs (as will IT, or other enablers), depending on cost, capabilities and timing.
- Where IT is involved, it needs to engage at the right level in the organisational hierarchy, in order to have the right information to drive the right decisions.
- Focused delivery using recognised programme and project management methods.
- Ensuring all parties clearly understand the deliverables the business considers are key, and that those involved can deliver them in a time-frame that meets the needs (often at the same time being pushed to drive down cost).
- Business must involve all parties at the business strategy road-mapping.
- Someone, somewhere, should be able to track the applicable metrics to validate the quality of work undertaken.
- Speed and execution!

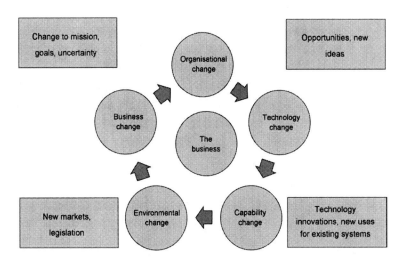

Figure 3: Inputs to change

High-impact change

Figure 3 provides examples of factors/issues that may be inputs to, or the cause of, change. And as discussed later in this chapter, it highlights IT as a major risk in change; as an area of the organisation that will in itself change, and also be a catalyst for change.

High-impact change affects the:

- Scope of a business: choosing to supply to different types of customer and markets; acquiring other business, or merging; privatisation, (new owners, new customer approach) and management buy-outs (new owners).
- Structure of a business: changing the business hierarchy and management controls through large-scale reorganisation.

- Core processes of the business: changing the way in which a business makes its products and services and delivers them to its customers.
- Culture (and therefore the organisation) of a business: implying changes in the behaviours and values held by the people working in the business, for example, changes in management style.

Businesses, therefore, must constantly deal with regular levels of change in the way in which they conduct their business. As discussed in Chapter 1, often these changes are enabled by IT, and IT is (nearly) always affected by business change. Some business managers contend that IT inhibits change. The business manager who is bringing about the change, or desires the consequences of the change, needs to be fully informed (indeed, accurately informed), in order to take whatever measures are necessary to ensure IT plays a positive role, during, and after, the business change.

They also need to be aware that changing the culture of the organisation, or the management hierarchies, or the domains within the business, may all be necessary in order to make change effective.

IT is indispensable ...

This book is not focusing solely upon IT; it is intended to draw attention to the way that IT has become integral to business. There is an argument for IT being indispensable to the business in every respect, though IT personnel need to recognise that the provider of the services may well be a cause for (business and IT) concern. The IT conceit that alignment to business is now irrelevant because of the integration, is predicated on an assumption that business will not change suppliers. IT is a commodity, nothing more; change to the organisation may well result from using IT, but IT, too, is subject to change within its own purview (as we mentioned earlier, because it sometimes appears to have been engineered without a blueprint), something that it has not managed too well. The good news is that not all IT change needs to be cumbersome. Change is easy to manage, if the IT components are well understood and good processes are in place.

Success probably depends on IT. You will need IT; yet IT problems can really stop your business operating effectively. So it might be a good idea to spend some time thinking about IT. In today's business environment, most managers realise that their business, and they themselves, are heavily dependent on IT. The overall importance of IT for administration, planning, marketing, communication, information sharing, service provision, production and research, is widely accepted. However, IT is there only as a service; it is important, but it is also important to look at IT in context. Figure 4 provides a context diagram. IT supports primary business processes, even where 'IT is for sale'. The primary business focus is the profitability of the business – which is enabled by IT.

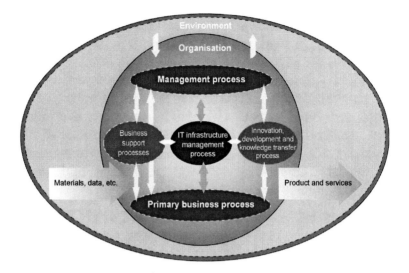

Figure 4: Context diagram for business and IT

Questions you might be asking yourself about IT in a time of change include, is IT:

- An investment to be capitalised?
- A major project risk?
- A pain?
- Responsive?
- A business benefit?
- A source of uncertainty?
- Out of control?
- An area of investment or divestment?
- A business opportunity?
- A source of innovation?
- A source of mystery?
- A sourcing issue?

Answering these questions will help to orient your thinking about what might need to change in IT to provide better support to the business.

Business goals

As mentioned in the first chapter, there are generic goals for an organisation that need to be fulfiled, and these can be classed as business goals.

Fulfiling the business goals is different, however, to classifying them. Businesses are not closed and shuttered systems, since any business influences, and is influenced by, its environment. The environment of the business comprises anything and anybody related to, but not part of, the business!

Change is typically brought about by the need to fulfil one or more of these generic business goals:

- To survive: if the existence of the business and the continuity of its identity are endangered, means of surviving will be identified.
- To prosper: if the business experiences declining prosperity, or expects this to happen in the future, it seeks ways to change, so that it becomes viable again.
- To benefit its stakeholders: when the business's stakeholders (or what those stakeholders value) change, the business needs to be changed to reaffirm the value of its existence.

Survival and prosperity are often defined in terms of the business environment, e.g. 'market leader' or 'benefiting the general public'. If the ability of the business to meet these goals is, or is seen to be, at stake, then the business, or, more specifically, the organisation looking after the business, and probably lines of business, will need to be changed, reinvented, renewed, or even created.

Adaptation of the organisation

The adaptation of a business to its environment, and vice versa, is a continuous process. If interaction with a changed, or changing, environment turns to conflict, it requires a major change programme, to ensure that interaction can still take place, and that the business remains prosperous. More drastic measures are then needed to realign the business with its environment, and that is the crux of what radical organisational change is about: dramatic measures through which the business is realigned with its environment. In modern times, this is mostly manifested as cost cutting, in itself mostly manifested by reducing staff, either directly, or by outsourcing jobs.

In order to deal with the consequential organisational change, you will need to consider myriad issues. These are some of the questions that you may have in mind:

- Do I have sufficient information?
- How much time do I have?
- When will the change take place?
- How many people are affected?
- What are the HR, legal and political issues?
- Is the timescale fixed or not?
- How many people can I involve in planning?
- Has a full risk assessment of the proposals taken place?
- What tasks can I delegate safely?

- Who is in charge of the programme of change?
- Will the change mean a change in business direction?
- What support processes will be affected?
- Will there be a change to my information needs?
- What technical support is available to help me?
- What technical changes will be required that need to be planned and integrated within the programme?
- What new capabilities are required from the IT infrastructure?
- Can the current IT infrastructure deliver what is required, or must I instigate technical IT changes?
- Can I insulate myself from IT failure?
- If not, how can I avoid IT failure?
- What is needed to ensure business continuity?

There are, of course, many other questions. However, making an attempt at 'knowing what you don't know', will help you to assess the uncertainty of the situation, which is one indicator of the scale of the problem. The management issue is one of programme management, and expertise to help you is available from many sources.

Surviving change

It is worthwhile spending some time considering the fundamental causes of change in business, and why some changes are easier to survive than others. Where the business is operating in a well-established niche, providing well-known products or services in a stable market, it is likely that IT capabilities are well matched to business needs. Changes are unlikely to be major, and should be (relatively) easy to manage and survive.

In such a situation, if the market begins to change, the relationship between the business and IT is probably reflected in the business and IS strategies for the future. In that case, IT will be an enabler of the changes and the business transformation. Although more risk is involved, survival is more a matter of good management and planning.

In situations where the business is operating in a stable market, and gaps are found between the business requirement for IT support and the IT capabilities that are available to the business, major change in IT is most likely necessary. The ability to survive is, to an extent, dependent on the scale of the change and the speed with which it has to be undertaken, but the risks can be controlled.

If, however, the capabilities of the IT organisation are not aligned with the business strategy, and the business capabilities of the business are not aligned with their market niche, then the business is presented with very significant challenges. The rush to provide Cloud services is a good example of radical, paradigm-shifting change. Business units began to procure IT outside of internal channels, forcing IT service teams to rush to build their own Cloud services, or attempting to become the go-between for business and Cloud providers.

A major risk is the almost total inability of technologists (rather than applications developers) to understand three things:

- IT services, as defined by technologists, are not the same as services as defined by the business.
- Technologists have little, or no, understanding of business processes and dependencies.

- The market in which the business operates (often addressed by appointing someone from the business side to the post of CIO).

To compound these issues, many (in fact, let's be controversial and say all ...) large legacy systems need wholesale re-engineering, in order to even make the applications suitable for being provided as Cloud services (and this is still ignoring major issues, such as security and privacy). This, of course, requires massive investment and a lot of time, both of which militate against the desire for speed and execution demanded by business, leading to more dissatisfaction with IT.

Why is IT so unresponsive?

Unresponsiveness is not always IT being either intransigent or arrogant. First, there is often a gap between the current business capability and the capability needed to ensure success in the market – see the bullet points above. Organisational change (probably involving IT to enable the business also to adapt to the required extent) is inevitable. Second, there is often a mismatch between the business needs and the ability of IT to provide the support. In this situation, IT is both a problem and a solution; and someone must initiate and manage an extensive programme of change that includes substantial changes to IT.

Facets of change management

As an organisation evolves, so should the business processes, and supporting IT processes, and the IT involved in it. Change is constant and chaos not far away. Some change requires massive management overhead (extensive programmes or projects), some can be automated – and then there is a range in between that comprises a spectrum of resource requirements, management attention and automation. In this section we will have a closer look at three aspects of the change process:

- What might be changed
- How you should go about getting it changed
- The interaction between the business and changes in IT.

Many people would like to believe that deciding what should be changed in the organisation's use of information technology is largely a technical matter. As the IT organisation's requirements change, should not the technical implementation of those requirements follow? Within acceptable time limits and budget constraints, of course.

Well, not really. Does the business care if IT wishes to move computing into the Cloud? They might not be too happy if IT decides to move from MS Office to Google applications – on the other hand, they might love those apps. They might also care if sensitive data is managed outside of 'internal IT' – irrespective of whether or not IT can procure cheaper computing power. The point is that IT is the tail, and the business is the dog – change is initiated by the business (the dog) and the tail had better wag when so instructed.

What if IT recognises that a major change programme is needed and that such change will not be instigated by the business? These next points are drafted specifically for people working in IT who perceive a need to make a change that impacts the business – and who recognise that IT does not own the business.

2: Why Change the Organisation?

First, make sure you can document and explain (in non-technical terms) the functional and technical requirements of changes to the organisation's IT systems – and why that is important to the business. Change makes people wary; it is, therefore, necessary to have made a comprehensive analysis of risks and a risk mitigation strategy. Changes in the organisation's requirements regarding IT, and the technical implementation thereof, will generally need to proceed in parallel. How will you guarantee business as usual?

Proposals to change the IT organisation, acquire IT assets, direct development of information systems/services functionality and regulate command over the flow of information, are among the items that will be negotiated with the business – with the business in charge of decision making. Do you know the degree of flexibility that you have in terms of deciding your own responsibilities for any proposed change? What financial limits do you have?

Proposals to change and decisions to change technical infrastructure and supporting organisation, will be formulated on the gap between perceived actual, and potential achievable value. Both values are largely determined by a mix of hard and soft value factors, such as cost, economic benefits, personal command, individual experience, prior investment, marginal improvement cost, resource consumption, in accordance with existing and desired mission and culture, etc. But that does not mean they will be accepted – what is the business case for the proposed change?

In summary, it is good practice to analyse and determine your position with respect to changes in business and in IT, if you want to have control over the changes:

- The technical and systems/services perspectives (consider presenting an IT portfolio analysis scheme, depending on the nature of the change, the type and scope of system, the role of IT and the required innovative capability).
- The personal and political perspectives (*see Chapters 3 and 4*).
- Your role in the decision-making process regarding IT.
- The risk perspective (Chapter 4).
- External and internal contingencies in your decision-making process on IT.
- The constraint perspective; focusing on a desirable outcome, whilst being confronted with the usual financial, organisational, geographical, social and timing limitations – moving to Cloud/virtualisation being entirely applicable here.

Before entering the labyrinthine bargaining and consensus processes of decision making, you need to determine what changes to IT you want to make, and what options are available to you. This is discussed further in Chapter 4.

IT change management and the organisation

What about change management as described in methods, such as the IT Infrastructure Library® – ITIL®? This needs to be put into context. Automation of changes at the infrastructure level should be simple to establish and a sound financial business case should be obvious. This can be the starting point for looking at change from the generic standpoint and establishing IT as the trusted adviser to the business. Keep in mind the business will have even less interest in ITIL® than they have in IT leading change. ITIL® is about managing the IT infrastructure and has no relevance to managing the business, or indeed as to how organisations should be structured (does anyone outside of the ITIL® dominion really believe that the ITIL® configuration manager, or the ITIL® change manager – in fact, any of the IT-centric roles defined in the framework, should sit on the Board of Directors?).

Programmes and projects cover a life cycle of change. ITIL® is not a best practice for either of these disciplines, and change management, as discussed in ITIL®, must always be put into its true context, as no more than a component of wider change management.

In the next chapters, we will discuss change issues in the context of why things change. We will also discuss where frameworks, such as ITIL®, are particularly useful, and where they have been misused.

CHAPTER 3: CHANGE ISSUES

Introduction

The beginning of this chapter discusses conditions, goals and the environment. Later, we move onto describing solutions and approaches.

When changing the organisation, irrespective of the reasons for change, IT is unlikely to be the first aspect considered to be a problem; however, many issues will materially impact on the IT infrastructure and applications running on that infrastructure – together these are the services consumed by the business (and the customers of that business) to run its business(es).

Consider the following:

- The change driver – why are we changing the business and for whom? Business in this context could be a service to the public provided by government, or by the private sector; new or revised social security or taxation legislation, for example, or new banking services.
- The scope and nature of the change – which parts of the business are to change and how (and why …)?
- What new, or altered, business capabilities are required?
- What changes in IT deployment are required to support these?
- How acceptable are existing IT systems and capabilities?
- What are the compatibility requirements of the new or altered IT systems, and is there an opportunity for

compromise, at least in the short term (in the instance of a merger or acquisition) (*see also Appendix 1*)? The last point is key – instead of a risky technical programme of change, can management (organisational) change be accommodated to allow parallel running?

- What architecture and design rules exist to govern the IT infrastructure post change, and what is the scope for transitional arrangements and compromises?
- What organisational and personnel issues affect the business, its use of IT, and its relationship with the IT providers?
- What is the current cost of IT and is it considered justifiable?
- What is the ability of the business and the IT provider (internal or external) to take the business and its IT from where they are now to where they need to be, in the required time-frame?

Other issues include competing for resources – generally resulting in projects competing for budget and increasing the time taken to get services to market (or the quality of services being delivered); varying degrees of maturity in terms of use of technology; trained personnel or processes being in place to facilitate both business and IT management – each of these points to an inefficient organisation. Often, the drive to reduce operational overheads, or to satisfy customers, leads to changes that were not properly planned or executed.

Six facets of the organisation

Consider Figure 5 for a moment and the allegory between changing the facets of a business and changing the alignment of the facets of a dice cube. Think of the cube as a well-known, trademarked puzzle!

Figure 5: The Perfect world

A business can be considered to have six major facets: strategy, process, organisation structure, technology, people and quality. Inevitably, someone or something, decides to change one of these facets because something – whatever 'it' is – is not working as it is perceived it should.

Maybe some nice, shiny new technology is needed by someone. And following changing out some old boring stuff for some new shiny stuff, things don't work quite as expected. The next step is to change the organisation to make it work better. Or, maybe the strategy. Or, perhaps educate our people because, clearly, they are the cause of the problem. Perhaps the quality of the work needs to be improved, so we implement a programme to instantiate a quality approach.

Inevitably, in a dice/cubes analogy, the result will resemble a manipulated cube – and getting things back together in the same way, will be an impossible task. The changes must (from a business perspective) be managed holistically.

The politics of change

A major component of any change, and one that is very often ignored, is the political climate of the business. Culture is more often than not a phenomenon of the prevailing political climate – that is both small and large 'P'. In Figure 6, if we consider that every business is a merchant of some flavour (even governments), then a number of major political elements can be recognised.

Figure 6: The political business

Any business created, and run, by its founder (usually then the CEO), will adopt the characteristics of the founder. Should the founder step aside, the way the business works will change, perhaps not immediately, but inevitably. Good examples include Apple and Microsoft. Where a founder takes all material decisions, it is very likely that an organisational structure will have been created to ensure that autocracy cannot be challenged. Many governments have been predicated on a system, such as this (and not all of them have fallen). Where these governments have fallen, the change (to democracy) creates its own challenges. Even a democracy is impacted by the nature of the governing body; not all democracies are the same and they reflect much of the nature of the leading political figure. The same is true of business change in such circumstances.

The way in which change is (or should be) managed is related strongly to the political ethos that prevails in the business.

For each quadrant of the diagram shown in Figure 6, the following dominant role models are described:

- The thought leader: these individuals seek an advisory role, with corresponding behaviour expected of people they work with (i.e. no ideas to be implemented 'off the shelf', adopt and seek to adapt ideas of others with more influence).
- The executive: this role is a decision maker, such individuals do not need to have ideas, it is expected that people will approach them with ideas and concepts.
- Coalition member: people with these characteristics lead through developing a common vision regarding change. They listen to, and incorporate ideas of,

coalition members and the opposition (anyone who has ever worked in the Netherlands will recognise this type of conduct, sometimes the drive to get everyone to agree leads to stasis, since no one wants to move forward without agreement). Consensus leaders look out for, and partake in, the coalition corresponding most closely to their own ideas.

- The merchant: this position is determined by the ability to focus on sales. People, such as this are alert to trade-offs and are content with a suitable compromise – whatever it needs.

These roles are present in different degrees in all leaders; many organisations have one particular influence that is prevalent and change is managed according to that dominant trait (see comment about the Netherlands).

Political issues are discussed in more detail in Chapter 4 (*see The political perspective revisited*).

Catalysts for organisational change

In the next sections, we will take a closer look at some IT catalysts for change. Why does change take place? Where does change originate?

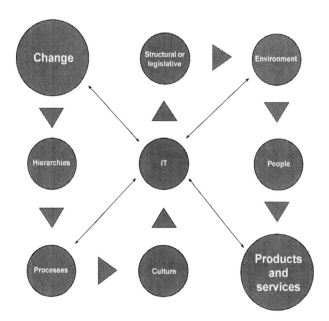

Figure 7: Change can be driven from many domains

The short answer is 'Anywhere' (see Figure 7). As we have mentioned, a current (white) hot topic is Cloud Computing; a major technology driver that is predicated on cost (or rather, less cost), but few have addressed one major cost issue – the cost of changing legacy systems that were designed to run on a specific platform and that are likely to be huge COBOL systems.

At this point, someone somewhere will cite their favourite method as being suitable for driving the associated organisational changes that will be an inevitable consequence of the brave new Cloud-world. Unfortunately, those 'someones' tend to be IT people who consider (for example) the ITIL® as the 'Bible' on any subject and blithely recommend an 'ITIL® compliant' organisation as the solution. And, because everyone wants change to be easy, it is not uncommon for the IT or ITIL® 'expert' to be charged with changing the organisation.

The words 'asinine' and 'risible' spring to mind, but, being politically correct, let's just say that it is somewhat misguided of IT 'experts' to expect to have IT leading the Board of Directors. This method of madness is also discussed later.

Legacy systems

Dealing with legacy applications is particularly pertinent to a period of organisational change, because the existing applications are what you start with. You would, no doubt, like to know how easily they can be changed and what they should be changed to. Various means can be used to assess how easy, or how difficult (and, therefore, expensive), it would be technically to change existing applications. You may also want to move your legacy systems to a new technical platform (think Cloud …), in accordance with perhaps plans for a new 'target' information systems architecture. In fact, various options are available to you for dealing with your legacy applications:

- Refreshment – modification of an existing system *in situ,* to address specific requirements or limitations, and to extend the life of the system.
- Conversion – transfer of the application from one IT platform to another, as mentioned above (bear in mind that re-engineering of some description will be needed).
- Re-engineering – the identification and extraction of business functions by analysing existing systems, and the generation of a replacement system in any

chosen technology (expensive, risky and time-consuming).

- Replacement – development of a new system to meet business requirements; the new system may replace some, or all, of the functions provided by the existing system.
- Replacement by the purchase of package software that has been built and proven by a third party; some element of bespoke development of software may also be needed to allow the package to meet your business needs.

The change issues are exacerbated by new technologies or the hype around new technologies. Cloud Computing, for example, is not really a new technology per se, unless it is a myth that business has been carried out over the Internet for the past 15 years. Cloud Computing is, however, a major driver for considering technology change to improve the ability of the business to control costs, and to innovate more rapidly.

It is also a cause of concern if all of the issues (for example the risks of changing platform, security issues, data ownership, cost of change, etc.) are not thoroughly addressed; the altered cube beckons.

Business goals

The ultimate IT goal is well-designed, architecture-conformant, integrated and flexible applications. From the business perspective, this is likely to be idealised as reliable, high-availability support from IT. The speed with which you move to this ideal will depend on the needs of your business. See Figure 8 for a list of the questions you may wish to ponder. If your priority is to have integrated and flexible systems, you will probably want to move faster than if your priority is to contain IT costs.

You will certainly want to make sure new applications are architecture-conformant, but you should decide what to do about existing applications on a case-by-case basis, depending on whether each application:

- Needs to be changed to meet business needs
- Is capable of being so changed
- Is worth changing to meet business needs and also, depending on whether, and how, each application can be accommodated on any new technical platform that is being introduced, to facilitate wider acceptance and increase use in the business.

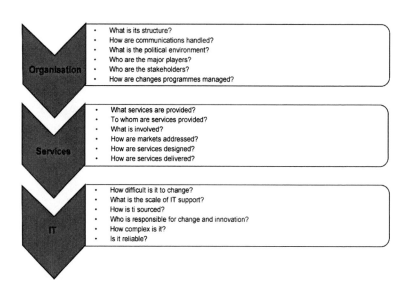

Figure 8: Questions

Replacement options

Development

A new system development allows total flexibility in terms of technology and design. Definition, construction and verification of the system carries the normal risks associated with application software development, which includes creeping scope and subjective judgement of correct completion. The risks to a development project are also greatly increased if data processed by an existing legacy system needs to be carried across to the new system. The wider the disparity of functions between the legacy and the proposed replacement systems, the greater are the costs and the risks. Partial redevelopment is possible, for example, to replace obsolescent user interface software.

Package

The solution of buying packaged solutions should be cheaper than an in-house development, because the development costs are shared across all potential purchasers. The migration of legacy data into the package, and the addition of any functional areas not covered by the package, can, however, substantially increase costs.

Choice of technology can be limited by the range of hardware/software environments in which the package is implemented. To avoid problems, purchasers should always ensure that the package has been designed for the technology on which it is expected to run, and is not converted from a disparate, technical platform.

Success, or failure, in package selection, rests with the purchaser. An accurate specification of functionality and supporting data structures by the purchaser will facilitate selection of an appropriate solution. Early consideration of the issues associated with the migration of business data to fit the package will significantly contribute to the successful implementation of a package solution. It is important to recognise that the more specific the customisation of a package that is required by the business, the less satisfactory this option will be and, in particular, the greater will be the costs and risks.

Approach to legacy software issues

Understand the asset

A comprehensive analysis of the existing IT application portfolio will result in an objective assessment of its strengths and deficiencies. It will also provide a template for assessing its appropriateness for the future.

Define business requirements

Prioritise the requirements for future changes and establish the timescales in which they must be achieved. Although requirements will inevitably change with circumstances, the degree of change in requirements should be kept to a minimum, because a moving target can frustrate the ambition of change.

Compare options for change

Examine the options for change to see which best satisfies the business requirements. A combination of options may be appropriate where different parts of your systems have different characteristics.

Perform a cost-benefit analysis

Having identified viable options, for each of these (including the 'do nothing' option), establish the costs and risks, and compare them against the benefits which will accrue to the business. The assessment should take account of the risks resulting from introducing new technology, extending functionality, or imposing restrictive timescales.

The cost-benefit analysis may suggest a different option for change than that initially considered to be the most likely. A change, of course, at this stage may save later embarrassment and expense, but is only possible with a comprehensive understanding of the legacy asset and environment, and an awareness of the range of options for change.

Changing the IT infrastructure platform

It isn't just the IT applications that you have to look at, the underlying IT platform infrastructure, comprising hardware, telecommunications facilities and supporting general purpose software, such as operating systems, may also need to be changed. Here are some of the questions to ask about the underlying IT infrastructure:

- Does it conform to a well-defined, up-to-date architecture?

- Is it capable of enhancement, to provide more capacity and to accommodate new applications?
- Does it support the levels of integration that will be required?
- Can it be regarded as mainstream, or is it obsolescent, or in a cul-de-sac?
- Does it, or can it, support technological innovation?
- Does it support current and foreseen needs for IT applications?
- Is it aligned with our longer-term thinking?

The ultimate goal can be further elaborated as a flexible, well-designed infrastructure that supports the integration of data and of applications, and that is based on a judicious mix of desktop, departmental, central and Cloud-based IT facilities, each of which adheres as far as possible to *de jure*, or *de facto* standards, or to available public specifications.

Wherever possible, new IT infrastructures should conform to the business architectural standards, but these must be flexible enough not to stifle technological innovations. Such new infrastructures need not be installed in a 'big bang', but gradually, over a period determined by the immediate and long-term needs of the business for IT support. It may be possible to build on the existing IT infrastructure in order to cope with the change.

Service delivery improvements

A major public service employer was examining approaches that would enable them to provide better services to the public. The major obstacle was considered to be the culture of the business, which was steeped in tradition and hierarchical structures. The following is a list of the elements that had to change in order to improve the service delivery processes. They decided to:

- Evolve a more outward looking culture
- Eradicate bureaucracy and tradition
- Use HR to reinforce required behaviours
- Improve internal communications
- Amplify the need for roles, rather than specific grades, within hierarchies
- Improve staff morale
- Examine how services were offered and described
- Improve the supporting processes (e.g. managing incidents and problems more effectively)
- Base organisational structures around the management of business processes
- Use IT to automate labour-intensive processes
- Deploy IT in a more strategic role, based on a new applications architecture
- Ensure that business goals were reflected in the new organisation
- Identify and quantify service demands
- Gear change proposals to meeting standards of service and negotiated expectations of customer's requirements
- Take into account, but not be constrained by, previous investments
- Require absolute, demonstrable commitment from the top.

A major change issue: Outsourcing

Outsourcing is a major change issue, with repercussions across all six elements of our organisational cube. Outsourcing is most often discussed in the context of IT, though it is no less often used for cleaning, HR, finance, logistics, security and many other services.

Outsourcing can be both an inhibitor of change and an enabler (depending upon perspective – and how well the contract was negotiated!).

Outsourcing – inhibitor of change

Over the years, it has been possible to collate a range of opinions about the possible benefits and risks of outsourcing.

Issues discussed included:

- Loss of professional IS/IT competence in the company
- Difficult to revert to in-house provision
- Ill-defined and ambiguous contracts, leading to disputes
- Little or no integration with corporate business
- Wasted time spent on disputes about costs, scope of contract, estimates, service quality, etc.
- Increased (even misplaced) dependence on the supplier
- Costs greater than anticipated
- Personnel unsettled
- Loss of flexibility, through being locked-in to the supplier's proprietary methods and tools

- Poor quality of software development; assistance required from within the company that was not anticipated
- Putative cost reductions in technology not achieved in reality because of long-term contracts
- Failure to recognise the need for specialist skills in contract management, contract negotiation and supplier management
- Managing contracts costs money and time, much more than originally believed
- Slow response to change
- Service levels
- Poor programme/project management, leading to delays and increased costs
- Profit takes precedence over business
- Complexity in managing both the outsourcing supplier and other third-party suppliers
- Long lead times before service quality is adequate
- Poor control of the contract exercised by both customer and supplier
- Unrealistic notions of the service levels negotiated with the supplier by the business and its end users
- Strangely, the business and its users dislike having to pay money for IT, especially to an external supplier – which leads to the question: why did they take that direction?

Outsourcing – facilitator of change

On the other hand, some customers of outsourcing suppliers of services cited a number of benefits that they believed were attributable directly to outsourcing:

- Immediate, effective application of professional standards
- Fewer people needed, fewer in-house specialists
- More cost-effective (and efficient) PC maintenance
- Problems often anticipated, leading to a reduction in major problems
- Smaller range of IT services requiring direct management
- Reduced bureaucracy
- Improved budgetary control
- A more customer-oriented IT service approach is often developed
- Business managers are free to focus on strategic issues, ensuring that they can focus on the needs of the business and less on the needs of users receiving a reliable level of service
- Business managers understand, and often value more fully, the contribution of IT
- Reduced total IT costs
- Predictable costs
- Faster services or systems development
- Developments delivered on time and to budget
- Third parties (e.g. network suppliers) find it easier to deal with changes through the outsourced IT supplier, reducing incidents, problems, delays and costs
- Users prefer to pay an external supplier rather than internal providers, because internal equates to free!

Some of the items appear in both of the lists; not surprising since outsourcing is an emotive issue and what one person considers a positive, another might consider a negative. The range of opinion will also be affected by where the individual sits (in or out of the organisation – maybe in or out because of the outsourcing).

It may appear to be anomalous, but it may also reflect the fact that a business spending more time on contract negotiations and using specialist advisers, obtains better results from outsourcing. Of course, even then the interviewees are blinded by their own preconceptions, good or bad. The reality, however, is that outsourcing is more successful if it is carefully planned and auctioned. In terms of IT, that is a lesson for those considering a move to Cloud services.

Consider again the cube analogy: small changes to one component find a way to becoming changes that cannot be foreseen. And, unlike the cube, you cannot find a key to put things back together.

Internal communications

Internal communication in times of change cannot be underestimated in terms of its importance. You need to have confidence that your personnel and contractors will understand why the change is being made, what is intended, and how they can help to bring it about. If you fail to communicate effectively, there is a major risk that people will thwart the change, rather than help to achieve it.

Branding a change programme to help with communications and to get people 'on board', is often a good idea. However, assuming that branding will solve all motivation issues, is not. By that, we mean that communications problems, once identified, are presumed to be easy to solve. Often change is managed at multiple levels, inadvertently creating tensions, false or unrealistic expectations, and the opportunity for disaster in terms of delivery. A good example is where organisations create executive sponsorship of projects (internal or external), delegating programme and project management appropriately, and then filling in resources at the coalface to do the necessary work.

At executive level, there is the desire to maintain a positive approach, to present the best possible picture of success. At the management level, this is met by selective presentation of information, not out of malice or even cowardice, but simply to maintain support. Often, issues or problems are discussed, but not sufficiently robustly, until the issue or problem has become a crisis.

Meanwhile, at the working level, there is increasing frustration that the management and executive level are failing to act on information that requires detailed attention, and action, in order to succeed. At this level, people become afraid of being scapegoated.

A project brand does nothing more than enable people to acknowledge a sense of ownership; it does not increase motivation, or change the way messages are passed through management layers. Of course, when things do go wrong, and executive management is forced to intervene, then often you will find that they look at how the project has been managed and then insert 'missing' good practices – obvious candidates being a communications plan where one did not exist, or a brand for the programme. Another regular intervention is the motivational speech featuring executives focusing on the wonderful opportunities, the valuable team members and how regular feedback sessions, led from the top, will get the programme back on track. Unfortunately, this does not solve the problem of no one wishing to be the bearer of bad news, until it is too late to act.

The tendency to optimism is a human characteristic that sadly leads to more inquests about 'what went wrong', then basic ineptitude. Further, the tendency at this point is to go into a full post mortem, project evaluation review, post implementation review – select your most used term – and the fickle finger of blame is pointed.

And then the workforce is vindicated in their fear of scapegoating.

None of the above is to suggest that executives, managers or workers lie, connive or deliberately conceal. It is simply a matter of fact that most change programmes that fail, do so because bad news is communicated either badly, or too late, or glossed over in the belief that hard work will make it go away.

We cannot solve this, but below you will see some of the questions to which you will need answers:

- What information (programme, project, goals, critical success factors (CSF), risks) do you need to communicate?
- How do we ensure that from the start, all possible problems and risks are documented, shared at all levels and a response recorded (*see The Agenda in Chapter 4*)?
- How will this document be tracked to ensure that issues are regularly reviewed, and that people are held accountable for decisions made about risks and problems?
- How can we ensure that information is focused, approved and endorsed business wide?

- Who are the decision makers?
- What are the target audiences?
- What do we want to achieve from this communication?
- When do people need the information?
- How can we provide the right information, at the right time to the right people?
- What is the most effective method of delivering the information?
- How will the results be measured?
- How will we know that the information has been understood?
- How can we ensure communications work two ways, giving and feeding back?
- Would discussion groups be effective?
- Can we use senior managers to illustrate commitment to change?
- Can they be held accountable for addressing risks and problems at an early stage?
- How much will it cost to communicate properly?
- How much will it cost if we fail to communicate properly?
- How many channels for communication exist in the business and is their use effective (in other words, is one forum for discussion better than a multi-tiered approach, and if not, how do we ensure that each tier addresses the same issues)?
- How do we continue the good practices post-change?
- What lessons have we learned that we will put into practice for the next change programme?

IT capability

If you are concerned about the capabilities of IT to deliver effective programmes of change, then that concern is probably wise. Ineffective IT is a ubiquitous problem and the statistics on successful IT projects are far from encouraging – but you can minimise the risks. If you have time, you may be able to do something with your existing IT in advance, to prepare it for the change. More likely you will have to prepare your IT during the change for the new business operations. In other words, your existing IT may not be a good starting point, but you will probably have to put up with that.

The quality of IT service provision can impact, positively and/or negatively, on:

- The smooth running of the 'old' business during the change
- The smooth introduction of the 'new' business during, and after, the change.

Business change will be successful only if the old and new businesses run smoothly, in accordance with the programme plan for the change. As far as possible, your IT should help you to achieve these objectives. You should certainly take steps to make sure your IT does not prevent you from achieving them.

To help you to understand the impact of IT on the business change, you will need answers to at least the following questions:

- Do we understand the strengths and weaknesses of our existing IT?
- In particular, what are our existing IT's change capabilities?

- What time do we have to get our IT ready to cope with the business change?
- Is there an IT architecture, or strategy, or blueprint which sets the direction for IT change in the business? Do we understand the IT changes that will be needed alongside the business change? What new capabilities are needed? What new systems? What changes to underlying IT infrastructures?
- Do we have a programme plan which sets out the milestones for IT change during the business change?
- Does the programme plan include provision for the smooth running of the old IT, as the new IT is phased in?
- Does the programme plan allow for risks to the programme? In particular, what contingency is there to allow for slippage in the timescales for IT change, or for IT projects that fail to meet expectations?
- Is the degree of IT resourcing realistic and achievable? Does the business's IT provider have enough of the right skills available?
- Are there enough funds for IT?
- Is there a fall-back position for each IT change? What can be salvaged if any such change should fail? Can we say which requirements can be deferred, or dropped, and which are essential if the IT projects get into trouble?
- What are the arrangements to make sure the business can assimilate the various IT changes? Who is responsible for making sure the proposed changes are acceptable to the business; for defining the new way of working; for testing the changes on

behalf of the business; for training the business users; for accepting the IT changes on behalf of the business?

- What arrangements are there for phasing out the use of the old IT by the business?

Dependencies

Where there are interdependencies between projects, or there is a likelihood of knock-on effects from one project to another, these should be clear in your programme plans. It is a responsibility of the programme manager to make sure these interdependencies and knock-on effects are properly managed.

The business environment may well change rapidly, perhaps in unpredictable ways during the change, or the objectives of the programme may change. Again, it is a responsibility of the programme manager to make sure changes to the programme are translated into changes to IT-related projects within the programme.

Preparing for the impact of change on both business and IT is concluded only after you have considered all of these issues. Only then will the 'new' IT be fully alerted to support the new business operations, or, at least, as close to being able to identify its definitive form as your planning deems appropriate.

CHAPTER 4: CHANGING THE ORGANISATION

Introduction

The diagnosis of the problems facing the organisation, and any ideas you might have to solve the problems, is one thing, but what next? It is certainly a good idea to simplify the task of changing the business and its IT in your mind. This means focusing on the key issues: upon the changes that are most important and those that are the most urgent. It means breaking the task into manageable components that deliver measurable benefits to the business. It means defining clearly what is to be done, when and by whom. It means allocating responsibility and ownership for business and IT systems and changes to the right person.

It may seem dumb, but let's keep in mind that computers are dumb; computers do only these basics:

- Automate repetitive, time-consuming tasks done by people – and save money; it may be old-fashioned, but some businesses will benefit from such a programme, perhaps because it is a while since automation was put in place.
- Help to eliminate bureaucracy, which is a key factor in efficiency – or lack of efficiency, again regular reviews of past change will be beneficial.
- Enable smarter working: a cliché, but teams which are enabled, with clear goals and appropriate technology, can work quickly, simply and directly.
- Simplify the flow of work: standard operations and maintenance recommendations to streamline interactions and smooth workflows can pay

enormous dividends by means of a refined data infrastructure, allowing you to get the right data to the right people, at the right time.

- Help to reduce unnecessary work through redesigned control procedures – a key governance issue.
- Allow you to find ways to bypass both internal and external bottlenecks by means of new technologies.

Computers do not replace meta-processes or processes, they replace procedures and provide support. That's about it.

So let us assume that you have already decided, or someone may have decided for you, the scope, scale, nature and purpose of the change in business operations that is to be brought about. This decision making corresponds to the programme identification phase (described in the OGC Guides to Programme Management).

Programme management

An enormous amount of good practice is now available about managing portfolios, programmes and projects, and risks. It is not the intention of this book to reinvent the material, just to make you aware of it, and how it helps in the planning of organisational change, and the change programmes that are part of that.

In the programme definition phase, it is necessary to define the programme in more detail; in particular, to develop the blueprint of future business operations and of the IT infrastructure that is to support the business, to solidify the business case for the change and to define the profile of benefits to be realised by the change.

Briefly, whether or not you adopt a formal programme management approach, at this stage you must:

- Agree the programme management organisation and procedures, to ensure the successful execution of the programme, in tranches if appropriate.
- Ensure good governance, by establishing a steering group with well-documented procedures for handling issues and risks (*see Internal Communications in Chapter 3*).
- Initiate communications that will ensure awareness and commitment of all affected personnel (*see Internal Communications in Chapter 3*).
- Define, in detail, the scope and interdependencies of all projects in the first tranche of programme execution.
- Document the detailed scope, objectives and plans of the programmes in a programme definition statement.

Key concerns for programme planning, as far as technology is concerned, are to make sure that the:

- Policies, service and system designs and processes that will achieve the required compatibility and flexibility of the business's IT systems in future, are adhered to.
- All specifications and requirements are well-defined and achievable.
- Speed and the degree of change can be accommodated and will not be overwhelming.
- There is a continuity plan in place to support the business, should IT become a cause of disruption.

- There is, at all times, a fall-back position to recover as much IT capability as possible, should changes go wrong.
- Business operations can carry on smoothly, by virtue of having satisfactory IT support, before, during and after the change.

Common issues in managing change

The goalposts of any change are not always fixed, as any change to the business is, typically, a response to changes in the organisation's environment – which just keeps on changing.

Hence, changes in the organisation's requirements regarding IT, and the technical implementation thereof, proceed in parallel. The necessary (but unwelcome) parallelism results in confusion and synchronisation problems regarding the business, for whose benefit IT is being changed (yes, IT is for the business, IT is not there to keep techies happy); it is also a major cause of project-creep and slippage. Being aware of this, and adopting strong programme management, will assist with keeping the change programme under control.

You may be a member of the dominant coalition in the organisation that is promoting a programme of change, but resistance to change will be persistent – as mentioned in Chapter 3. Change makes people wary – and resistance will inevitably be influential. Any decisions regarding how to deal with resistance will necessarily be made in flight. It may be as simple as issues being raised about the hardware needed to support computing power, estimates needing to be revised, or something as complicated as a fundamental rethink of development because new service development is running over budget.

Proposals, then, might be required to change either, or both, of the business and IT organisations, acquire different IT assets, direct development of IS functionality (applications development or redevelopment) and reconsider how to communicate.

Last, but not least, proposals to change, and decisions to change technical infrastructure and its supporting organisation, will be formulated on the gap between actual and potential achievable value. Simply put, unless the business investment in new infrastructure demonstrably pays positive dividends, why would they make the investment?

Changing IS and IT

As we discussed in Chapter 3, changing technology support is an issue for the majority of organisations, and where change is business led, there are particular factors that the business should take into account. For example, prior to entering any decision making, you must determine what changes to IT you want to make, and what options are available to you (have another look at Figure 2 and consider again the discussion about Outsourcing in Chapter 3).

This is an analytical process which can be approached in a structured fashion:

- Analyse the areas of IT where the organisation needs to make changes.
- Establish the extent of changes that will be made by the organisation to each area that is likely to change.

- Compile a comprehensive document of required changes (organisation, people, process, technology and cultural).
- For each likely change, find out what goals the organisation will want to achieve as a result of the change.
- For each likely change, identify risks and rewards.
- For each likely change, create a business case.

Construct a table of how the change (scope, structure, process) affects:

- Services to the business
- Services within IT
- Systems management
- Support
- Primary processes
- Support processes
- Innovation and development.

It is also important to consider the life cycle of change. When it comes to thinking about the services that the business needs to function, the following can be a useful means of categorisation:

- Embryonic (the service has to prove potential)
- Emergent (has potential but needs a foothold)
- Static (has to grow)
- Established (is used widely)
- Established (is unreliable!)
- Rarely used (is as good as dead).

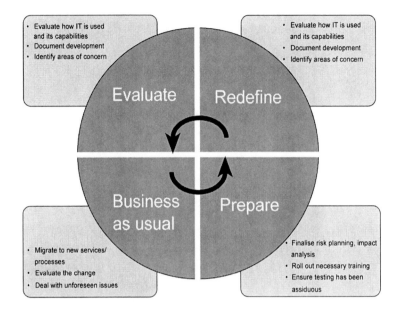

Figure 9 Business led IT change

Look at Figure 9 from the business side, you should consider IT as a strategic asset, one that if changed will result in organisational changes predicated on making IT more useful. In essence, you are evaluating the role of your IT (also competences and capabilities), redefining its role according to need, preparing the entire organisation for change, and then – with luck and good management – returning to business as usual, albeit with (hopefully) improved services and capabilities.

Determine organisation-wide objectives of changing a particular item. Look at the future business value of the IS/IT systems and services, if necessary. Verify selected dominant change mode versus skills and resources required to make the change. If a gap in skills, capabilities or resources appears, ask the obvious question – Can it be done?

If the answer is no, then it may be necessary to reconsider what is to be changed, or to examine the organisational changes necessary in order, simply, to get change moving.

It is important to assess the effect of changes to the business organisation for which you are responsible, and to decide if the change is truly innovative, if the change is an improvement, or even if the change has no impact, or worse, it is possible to identify negative impact. In a nutshell, do you like the change and can you make it work?

Determine your stake in changing an IS/IT system or service (e.g. minimise risk, conserve resources, stimulate innovation, speed up (or slow down how business is enacted), increase certainty, etc.) with respect to the rational criteria of costs, financial benefits, response and delivery times, productivity, effectiveness, continuity, flexibility, etc. Determine desirable and (perhaps, barely!) acceptable levels of performance.

All of these criteria will be important in making sure change is managed effectively, with appropriate manageable impact on the various organisational domains.

The political perspective revisited

In Chapter 3 – The politics of change, we outlined some of the political perspectives and promised to revisit the issues in more detail.

Inevitably, there will come a time when decisions need to be made on the nature of the change(s) and how it/they will be managed and implemented in the organisation. Where IT is a dominant feature of the change, business should be represented in considering how both sides of the organisation may have to change. To be an effective participant in the decision-making process on IT, you should ask yourself three questions:

- Who makes the decisions on IT?
- How are decisions on IT made?
- What is my role in the decision-making process?

Since nobody really makes decisions with potentially severe business consequences on their lonesome (except maybe one or two Warlords, or the odd Dictator), there must be a platform on which such decisions are made. The usual platform for decision making can take a variety of forms (especially for IT; the UK Government, for example, has a formal and well-documented means of engaging IT – though not necessarily a successful one – IT and information systems projects remain complex, difficult to manage and consistently gather less than glowing headlines, hence the discussions in this book), examples of good practices to manage change include:

- Formalised committee in the organisation, such as 'IT Executive Committee', 'Infrastructure Planning Committee', 'Information Steering Group', or similar.
- Formal committees based on good practice in programme and project planning methods.
- A level in the organisation's hierarchy, such as CIO, Group IT Director, Head of Division, etc.
- Less satisfactory, but better than nothing, an ad hoc group of interested managers, or a combination of individuals that feel they need to, or must, have a say on the subject.

Whatever the shape of the usual decision-making platform, it must have the characteristic that the decisions made are actionable decisions, not ratifications. In times of major change, if IT is not considered to be of strategic importance, then the strategic decisions tend to be made higher up the organisational ladder, without regard to IT. In such instances, IT decisions will be made outside of these formal/semi-formal bodies (perhaps within IT, without discussion elsewhere), as the customary business decision makers have more pressing matters to attend to.

Such a decision to delegate what is, in effect, high-risk decision making, to an important but nonetheless ill-equipped body, is not necessarily a sound move, given the ubiquitous nature of technology. Business and IT must be aligned in the decision-making processes, with business leading and IT making informed suggestions.

If you are (or should be) a concerned decision maker; that is, you are a stakeholder in ensuring IT fully supports your part of the organisation, you should investigate your position with respect to the usual decision-making platforms: Are you a member? Would you like to be? Can you overrule the usual decision makers?

For any issue or problem to be drawn to the attention of the decision makers, an issue must be on the agenda. The decision-making agenda, like the platform, can take a variety of forms:

- A formal list of defined events and issues that must be brought forward
- A list of topics for a meeting
- At worst, personal mental notes of decision makers.

Once more, good practice guides in programme and project management, and in risk and portfolio management, can be used to help inform you of what you should do. No composition will be (or can be) perfect. To be effective, a senior management representative is, however, just about mandatory, and keep in mind that too many directors can lead to political issues that will hinder effectiveness.

The agenda

In many organisations, the agenda was long ago kicked to the old-fashioned fence, because new IT services allowed the impatient to manage using PowerPoint slides and e-mail. The very idea of religiously noting actions and following up on progress was amusing, since electronic toys could do that without actually having to think about management.

Of course, the agenda and following up items on the agenda is old-fashioned and it is tedious, but electronic aids do not dispense with need, they support proper use. Agendas are an important instrument in the decision-making process. An agenda allows:

- Individual concerns to be drawn to attention, or, to gain the opportunity to be heard.
- Concerns to be recognised as an issue, in other words, to transform individual concerns to concerns of the organisation.
- The opportunity to explore several approaches to resolving the concern. If there are no options, then there is no decision to be made.
- Focus on the process of gathering relevant information from multiple sources.

- Trade-offs among concerns, issues and approaches.

The use of agendas in communications is underestimated. Decision making almost never takes place on a single, individual issue, but rather is based (or should be based) on the entirety of issues. Taking part in the decision-making process implies that you are in touch with the right platform and the right agenda. In summary, are you one of those who can:

- Suggest changes (for example, regarding IT)
- Influence what appears on the agenda
- Withhold consent on changes
- Provide information on changes
- Suggest approaches
- Help decide what will be done.

Your role in the process of decision making

Once you know your personal position in the decision-making process, all that remains is the question of how to apply yourself most effectively in the process.

There are two principal factors:

- The dominant political system within the organisation (mentioned in Chapter 3 – The politics of change)
- Effective personal influence.

The role you adopt in the decision-making process is influenced by the politics within the organisation. Politics, not in the 'House of Commons/US Senate-oh-no-not-them' sense of the word, but in the utilitarian sense of 'the manner in which differences in opinion and interest among groups and persons are resolved'.

The first influence, the dominant political system, pertains to the way in which the organisation predominantly reaches decisions. And as mentioned in Chapter 3 – The politics of change, if you have a CEO that makes all the decisions, the rest of this is just words.

There are a range of political systems in any organisation, and a wider range of characteristics. Some of the more common ones are mentioned in the next section. Think about how your organisation works, by matching with the most obvious characteristics in the lists. The lists are (as with all such lists) guidance and are not intended to be definitive.

Dominant political system characteristics

Autocratic

- Centralised on one individual
- Clear hierarchical structure
- Worker task specialisation
- Rigid chain of command
- Formal decision making

Feudal

- Centralised on committee structure
- Ambiguous top level structures
- Specialised tasks
- Rigid, overt, loyalty-based command structure
- Decisions made informally and ratified formally

Mixed

- Mix of centralised and decentralised committees
- Matrix management structure
- Hierarchical, with most large projects and programmes within silos
- Ambiguous chain of command
- Ambiguous decision making

Participative

- Decentralised
- Numerous well-managed team and project structures
- Versatile workers
- Delegation of authority to workers
- Many programmes and projects based on working across boundaries
- Visible professional and personal commitments

Organic

- Completely decentralised
- Flat structure
- Generalist workers
- Workers choose managers (and vice versa)
- Strong on vision and values
- Boundaries absent
- Informal culture.

By focusing on organisational political characteristics and understanding that the manner you employ when you wish to be part of decision making will, to an extent, depend on your displaying characteristics that identify you as part of the culture, it will be easier to get your opinions aired –

though not necessarily actioned. Remember the point about the characteristics of the CEO.

The risk perspective

Major changes within organisations are inherently risky and engender upheaval, unsettled people and unstable systems and services. Whenever an organisation undergoes a major change programme, it is taking chances with its future. If the change is a huge success, the organisation will prosper; if the change programme is a washout, the organisation will have spent too much energy and will find it difficult to survive.

As necessary (and as regular) as change in business may be, the same necessity does not apply to the detailed changes of the inner workings of the organisation resulting from the change. Neither the need for changes, nor the willingness to take the corresponding risks, is likely to be as high as for the change in itself. For example, an insurance company might wish to create a mobile claims service in order to compete better in the market and will spend a lot of money to make the change programme work. The same amount of time and money would not necessarily be spent on IT support, bringing in new staff, re-engineering major applications and creating a new management structure to align IT service provision with lines of business. More likely, there would be an expectation that the organisation would not require change because the change impact would be restricted to tinkering with a few wires and one or two computer boxes.

In the following paragraphs, we will discuss the risks involved in changing, or not changing, the organisation's IT capability, with a view to achieving the goals of proposed business change.

So, you reasonably might ask, what are the risks and are they really relevant? Consider a change that has implications for the reward system of an organisation; one incorporated in a performance management system operated by HR. To effect the change, the software for the payroll application has to be modified. This modification is a complete failure and almost everybody receives the wrong salary; let's say they receive substantially less than expected – most people would not be concerned by receiving more – though the point here is that there is a fundamental impact on the personnel in the entire company.

Taking the decision not to change the IT capability can have similar consequences. Consider the case of a manufacturing company that changes its plant production process, so that it would be able to produce goods in small batches, but decided against the replacement of any machine time scheduling programmes which had been designed to optimise output on long production runs. The goals of the change which would likely have been lower stock levels, greater diversity of products and increased responsiveness to demand, would simply not be achieved.

To initiate changes in the IT capability in order to further the goals of any proposed change, requires that you consider the possible consequences and take appropriate countermeasures. You should identify a particular approach to managing the risks associated with changing, or not changing, an area of the IT capability. The following terms outline the dominant risk management behaviour and provide a checkpoint for thinking about countermeasures; they are the basic, fundamental concepts of managing risks:

- Risk avoidance: aimed at decreasing the relevance of a risk to the proposed change.
- Risk protection: aimed at deflecting the potential vulnerabilities to affect the change.
- Risk mitigation (damage limitation): aimed at countering negative consequences of risk on the radical change.
- Risk confrontation: aimed at meeting the risk head on, taking the chance, sometimes known more simply as risk acceptance.
- Risks pertaining to changes in the business use of IT can be applied at two levels:
  o The global level in which the risks, due to the organisation's environment (legislative changes, growth and decline, competition, etc.), are considered.
  o The risks due to the organisation itself (strife, confusion, responsiveness to change, capability and technology) are explored with respect to the IT capability as a whole. This exploration should lead to an understanding of the contribution of IT to the failure factors of achieving the goals of change. Countermeasures, such as the damage limiting policy to allow open-ended or framework contracts for the provision of IT services or specialist manpower in the case of uncertain volume, or using on-demand IT provision, can then be identified and suggested.

There are several viable groupings for risks. This discussion is largely separating the issues between extraneous and inherent risks. As ever, it is not possible to be definitive in generalising these points and it is up to you to decide the valid, meaningful groupings and descriptions.

A constraint perspective

For more information about the *Theory of Constraints* books by E.M. Goldratt should be consulted. In the next few paragraphs, a much simplified discussion about some constraints to action is considered. As much as we would like to be in a position where it is possible to do everything, in reality we are not. And especially in times of change, the everyday constraints of time and money limit us in what we would like to achieve.

Having mulled over and discussed what you need to do, how badly you want it, and how you can gain commitment, it is now time to descend to the mundane matters of resource allocation. And anyone who has descended to that knows just how difficult it is to identify and schedule resources. Just one more constraint is how often the same names come up every time a 'Tiger Team', or new project, is identified.

Strange how there is never a 'Fluffy Bunny Team'.

People's time is a valued resource in any organisation and especially when the business organisation must undergo many changes, whilst it keeps on doing what it normally does. It is extremely important to keep on top of resource issues, particularly where the organisation needs to bill resources and balance billing with internal investment.

In summary, resources (people), time, quality, money, ability to absorb change, appetite for risk and availability of key skills, should all be considered as possible restraining influences.

Responding to change

A major factor in the successful operation of any business is its ability to respond to changing circumstances. Effective harnessing and exploitation change, whether or not it involves IT, or is driven by it, will depend on an appropriate response to continuous developments within the following three categories:

- Changes in the environment in which the business is placed
- Advancements in technology
- Changes in the business organisation that makes use of the IT technology/infrastructure.

Thus, even a well-constructed programme of change will be directly influenced by the ubiquity of change in the business environment, the improvements in technology support and (less frequently) the desire to adapt IT to accommodate organisational change in the business.

These ongoing developments, probably better described as opportunities (or some would say threats), can happen at any time before, during, or after the change – but be cautious about always looking to move the goalposts. If you alter the scope of your programme or projects, you will have to change one, or all, of the cost projections, the resourcing projections, or the agreed timescale, or at least re-prioritise the order in which you do things. In particular, it is not possible for your IT provider, internal or external, simply to absorb more work, without material impact on cost, quality of delivery or timing. Effective management, both during and after the change, will depend on an effective command and control structure in the business. For example, if communications are inadequate, management information about the change may go missing, or arrive too late to support decision making (see the next section for more transition issues). If that information concerns, say spiralling costs, how can prompt remedial action ever take place?

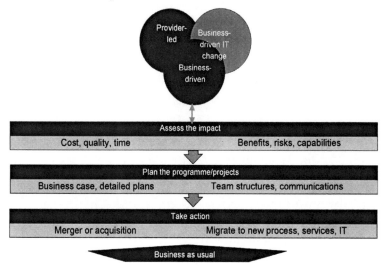

Figure 10: IT change

Figure 10 illustrates our discussions that IT change might stem from:

- The business: through a change in business requirements (perhaps caused by a legislative change, such as altering taxation rules).
- A business-led change to IT (perhaps the in-house IT provider is to be replaced by an outsourcing company).
- The service provider (e.g. where use of new technology is either being sought, or has been decided). In this instance, the service provider is assumed to be internal, since it is not common to

find external suppliers being the driver of business change).

Planning issues

For the selected option, prepare project plans covering detailed management activities.

Four principal steps (shown in Figure 10) are essential and are common to the planning, control and, therefore, survival, of an IT infrastructure transition that may accompany the changes mentioned previously. The steps are:

- Assess the impact of the change
- Plan the change
- Migrate to the new IT infrastructure/new IT applications/new business processes
- Return to 'business as usual'.

The satisfactory completion of an IT-related change will depend on diligent management of each of the steps above. If you have followed our guidance so far, you should have handled the first two steps satisfactorily and be ready to complete steps three and four.

Once you have implemented your IT infrastructure changes, there is no guarantee of stability. It is not just a matter of letting the changes settle down either. Because the lifetime and capability of any existing IT infrastructure (capacity, adaptability, size, reliability, area of deployment, etc.) is limited, it is likely that discussions about required new business capability, or about the opportunities for harnessing technological advances, sooner or later will result in a decision that further change is needed and justified. Therefore, both the business and the IT provider will need to survive a series of IT infrastructure transitions. Throughout, the business manager's challenge is to ensure the business obtains the greatest benefits from IT infrastructure change at the least risk and as cost effectively as possible.

Migration to new business systems or processes, and associated IT, depends on the business being ready to accommodate the new systems. IT and the business must work together to ensure the business is ready for IT change. This preparation involves basic planning actions, which, although mundane, are absolutely necessary, including:

- Identifying new jobs, competencies and the organisational command structures required
- Acquiring any new services or facilities required (e.g. training)
- Developing process manuals
- Developing testing packages and acceptance criteria for checking that new systems are aligned with the business expectations
- Developing training packages
- Signing off all plans and schedules to ensure they are acceptable to the business
- Integrating any new IT infrastructure and new business processes
- Testing the entire new process
- If parallel running with existing processes is intended, planning the cutover.

No doubt you have realised that all of these steps apply in equal part to changes that have impacted the business areas. Substitute one or two business service identifiers and the same list applies!

Business manager considerations

The IT-savvy business manager would be wise at this time to think about a couple of issues that should lead to them asking one or two pertinent questions:

- How much control do I need to retain and how much should I delegate? (This decision is largely dependent on a number of related factors: the scale of the change, criticality, quality of planning, the clarity of objectives and responsibilities, and the effectiveness – and nature, insourced or outsourced, of the IT providers.)
- What should be in the transition plan, so that I can be confident of the outcome?
- What are the principal indicators of whether we are getting anywhere with the plans? (Largely identifying missed deadlines or milestones, implementations fraught with problems, frequent discussions about reverting to trusted versions of software, the invocation of regression plans, perhaps even miserable faces in the programme team – this last one is not as uncommon as you may think!)
- Think about how you may be able to speed things up – or slow things down? (If you are paying for the work, you can include time penalties for failure to deliver on external suppliers, but don't forget that you would probably prefer the change to be implemented effectively, rather than obtain financial redress).

If you are working to a deadline, you might want to descope the scale of the change, to deploy additional resources, or to get help from contractors. You might prefer to pay a bit more to implement your changes on time, and to your requirements; it might also be possible to allot business personnel to the project as a resource for the provider. If things are moving too fast, it will be necessary to redraw project plans to reflect the changed requirements of the businesses.

Responsibility for drawing up the plans to change the IT infrastructure, will usually be delegated to the IT service provider. The business manager must ensure the interests of the business are taken into account in the plans.

Transition planning (and issues involved in the activity) is discussed in Chapter 4 – Transition Issues. At this juncture, we wish to make the point that any transition plan produced by the IT service provider should contain at least the following:

- A description of the current, and future, situation (including a 'blueprint' of the new IT infrastructure) highlighting the changes
- An overview of the advantages and disadvantages of the transition
- Schedules, timescales, costs, funding, allocation of resources (staff, contractors and other providers)
- A testing scheme; procedures, performance and acceptance criteria, responsibilities, parties involved, time issues, milestones, etc.
- The major dependencies and risks identifying contingency arrangements
- Rules and responsibilities.

The transition plan should be endorsed by the business manager, once assured that disruption to the business will be minimised and that there is a regression plan (or backout plan) should things go awry. Business managers should assure themselves that the regression plans are viable. Where practical, these regression plans, ideally, should be tested prior to implementation. It is good practice for the business manager to assess what business can be sustained without IT services, in the event of major problems, and for how long. It may be possible to design and test manual processes to be used in the event of failure in the IT processes; the migration plan should make appropriate reference to them.

Choosing when to implement IT-related change is essentially about finding a balance between the meeting of business needs and the avoidance of risk. On the one hand, the business may need new IT capabilities quickly, or by a certain date. On the other hand, it is better not to disrupt key IT systems at times of critical business processing.

Implementation tactics

The tactics selected for implementation of the change have an important bearing, both on the satisfaction of business need and on the containment of risk. In particular, a phased implementation can help with both. New IT capabilities can be brought in more quickly than with a 'big bang' approach. The risks are spread among a series of smaller, more manageable changes, with smaller, less risky, backouts needed if things go wrong. It is not always possible, or practical, to introduce incremental changes in accordance with strict business priorities – it also depends on technical and organisational feasibility – but at least the change can be organised, so that the business reaps the benefit of the new IT capabilities at the earliest opportunity. Also, stability can be restored on an incremental basis, rather than waiting for a 'big bang' which could, in turn, be just that.

Customer satisfaction

As new business systems and their supporting IT are tested, you need to decide what to do if you are not completely satisfied. You have the choice of putting up with what you have got, if you can live with it. This may be the best solution if the business change is time critical; you can always improve the system later. Alternatively, you can take a bit longer and get a system that is closer to what you really want, even if it costs you more, which is quite possible. This is a better solution, if the system you are rejecting falls significantly short of what you need. Take care of any knock-on effects. As an example, it may not be too serious if a new version of a current system is a few weeks late, but it could be disastrous if a new financial system is too late for the new business year.

It is vital that measurement criteria created for gauging the success of the radical change remains in place throughout the transition and beyond. The most important criterion is usually the realisation of business benefits, but you might wish to consider the deployment, or acceptability, of IT on the part of the business.

It must be anticipated that plans will not be set in concrete; timescales most likely will extend. At every stage of the change life cycle and beyond, the business manager must be aware of projected costs, benefits, risks, and of the options available, should problems be encountered. The business manager must be prepared to take decisive action, including instigating a fall-back to standby arrangements, whenever serious problems are manifest. Equally, if new opportunities arise, the business manager should be prepared to assess these and to change plans, if appropriate. But beware: you cannot simply take on further change without affecting your existing plans. Do make sure you understand the impact of seizing new opportunities, before you make your decision.

Before long, say in a matter of weeks, it should start to be clear whether the business and its supporting systems are working well enough. Not that the business will necessarily believe it if things are less than ideal. For a start, everyone is probably a bit fatigued by change and glad to be over the worst. The last thing tired people want is more problems. Not just that, the whole idea of the change was to make things better, or at least to make them work in the face of a difficult business environment, so in a sense, problems are unexpected. Radical change usually needs to happen quickly; problems that slow it down are not welcome. However, all change involves some risk and risks do, at times, turn into problems.

Business as usual

The lower part of Figure 10 mentions business as usual. It is important to log and manage problems with business systems and IT, in order to ensure as speedy a return to normal as possible. An organised approach to problem management will help with decision making, if the programme does not turn out to be a total success.

For example, if after two months you suspect your new billing system is not working satisfactorily, to the point that it is putting the business in jeopardy, it would be best if you had problem statistics on which to base your judgement about whether to abandon the system, or try to fix it, or revert to some previous arrangement, or call in contractors to help you out. You will want to know as soon as you can whether the business is benefiting from the change in the way you had expected. If you made the realisation of benefits an integral part of the change programme, you should find that the improvement is easy to measure, or at least to assess. The assessment may not be possible for some weeks, however, because inevitably, systems will have to be debugged or fine tuned, personnel will have to learn the ropes, and so on.

The period of grace cannot be allowed to go on for too long. The business needs to see benefits from the change; it is against the performance of the business that the change should be judged. So the problem management system needs to focus increasingly on issues that adversely affect the performance of the business and the effectiveness of the change. Once again, the outcome could be unpalatable: abandonment of systems, reversion to previous arrangements, further radical change, elongated timescales, descoping of the change – or it may just be a matter of improving processes, training or management.

These early weeks and months can be difficult. You cannot be sure in advance that your changes will work. You cannot even be sure that testing will find all the problems. Once the change has happened, you can judge whether it is working in practice and you can take action if it is not. You are allowed to be pragmatic: to accept what you can live with if your ideal is not met, to prioritise problems according to how serious they are, to take longer about the change if the business can stand that, perhaps even to spend more time on it; if by doing so you get a better outcome for the longer term.

Above all, do not fall into the trap of thinking that the change is over upon 'implementation'; until you are completely satisfied you can live with the outcome, and that could be several months after the change itself has been declared complete, you cannot sign off on the programme. Make sure that your provider understands that 'perfect' IT is not the goal of business change – you want an effective business system.

Once you are sure that stability has returned, keep scanning the business and technical environment; you may have to instigate more change sooner than you think.

Transition issues

Concluding with 'all is well' is something of a cop out. Things will go wrong and here we discuss some of the issues that might arise.

As discussed above, transition planning is, or should be, a key part of planning. Often, it is not given sufficient attention in planning because the motivation to get with changing something, far outweighs the motivation to ensure that any transition in the future (which is far, far away) goes well. Sometimes, transitioning is (attempted to be) addressed by creating artificial deliverables – the 30-day plan, the 60-day plan, the 90-day plan, and so on. Too often, these plans are predicated on a perceived need to demonstrate short-term 'quick wins', rather than to genuinely identify milestones that are useful and meaningful. The project management focus then causes attention to be diverted from longer-term risks and problems that should be addressed, to focus on short-term obstacles to satisfying the '30-day' deliverable – or whatever.

Transition planning should be part of any deliverable planning; by addressing what the impact will be of short-term deliverables, it is more likely that the transition planning will throw up more important considerations.

Slicing up a programme, or project, into bite-sized pieces is entirely correct; however, the nature of the slicing and the planning of the overall deliverables, and how all of the pieces will transition into a smooth programme of change, is much more important. We have been discussing how IT is just about inextricably linked to business change; thus your programme and project transition plans must take account of the impact on IT, of the way in which the change will affect your IT, and the way your IT will affect the change.

The most important thing to safeguard is the continuity of your existing IT support, which must be protected at all costs until the revised arrangements are in place – this might mean parallel running (expensive, but very often necessary to mitigate risk). You will have to build in regression (fall-back) arrangements and make sure you understand the business implications, should it be necessary to defer cutover to a new IT infrastructure, or new services and systems, in the event that you encounter problems.

Pay special attention to any existing IT systems upon which your business may be dependent, for example, your billing system. If you are happy with these systems, it is advisable not to change them, if you can possibly avoid it; you will have your hands full with other things and you can't afford to have your attention diverted fixing something that isn't broken. Guard against any deterioration in the support you receive from existing systems; changes in the environment, such as a loss of personnel and their tacit knowledge, can cause problems even where systems are otherwise unchanged. The best advice is to look at all systems that are critical to the business, assess the impact on them of all known changes, and plan and implement countermeasures to ensure any disruption is kept to a minimum.

If you are unhappy with existing systems, you will have to change them, but you must decide whether now is the right time. For example, you may feel that your current billing system is inefficient and that you need to replace it because your business is undergoing a radical restructuring. Once again, you may have your hands full, in this case with the restructuring. You need to be confident that you can handle the change of billing system, because you will not be rewarded for a new system that fails to work.

A phased approach to the business change, with the new billing system deferred until after the restructuring has settled, and an effective fall-back arrangement, would significantly reduce your risks.

A useful checklist for the transition planning would include:

- Who is responsible for the success of the programme and its individual projects?
- What are the roles and responsibilities, and who is responsible for business, user and IT issues, including IT design?
- Who is responsible for specifying IT requirements: does the business have enough control?

- Do we have enough IT personnel with the right skills, to run our existing IT and bring in our new IT? If not, can we can buy them in?
- Do we have enough IT funding? Can we cater for parallel running of old and new IT?
- How are new systems and infrastructure to be integrated into the ongoing operation? What are the testing arrangements? How can we check that business gets the new IT needed?
- What are the arrangements for decommissioning the old IT infrastructure?
- If the IT changes don't work, or can't be implemented smoothly, what fall-back arrangements are available and who is responsible for them? How confident are we that they will work?
- What arrangements are there to support the users with the changed IT? Will they work?
- Throughout the change, do we have a process for dealing with modifications to the change programme? Do we have a process for dealing with problems that arise?

CHAPTER 5: SIZING AND BUILDING THE ORGANISATION

Introduction

Organisational sizing and building is not necessarily a complex task, the problem is that to do it well, it is very time-consuming and labour intensive and, particularly in the era of immediate gratification (or, at least, the expectation of immediate gratification, with life being lived over handheld devices), anything that looks like hard work is either dismissed, or there becomes a belief that a short cut will exist that will make all the hard work go away.

Such thinking leads to acceptance (or rather a sort of rabid blind faith) that a method exists to wave a magic wand over big problems. In the world of IT, many 'religious' cults have existed that purported to own some magic elixir that would erase all worldly woes, or worse, become 'the next big, life-changing event that everyone would use and IT would rule the world'. The business world (unfortunately for the IT world, where new 'life-changing' cults are embraced every other year) tends to have a longer memory and, for some inexplicable reason, does not always get on board with IT radical thinkers.

According to many experts, it is possible to use ITIL® as a way to build an organisation. Given that ITIL® is an excellent method/framework for designing processes in the IT world, it seems odd that so many people put faith in the ability of consultants to use that guidance in an entirely different context. We often hear a question along the lines of *'How many change managers does ITIL® say I need?'*,

or *'How many service desk operatives does ITIL®
recommend?'*

Depending on the person asking (some people in the Deep
South of the USA carry guns ...) the answer varies from
'How would I know?', to *'11'* (followed quickly by *'No,
make that four, wait a minute, how about six?'*), or most
often, *'Depends – What do you want them to do?'*

The point is that any method you might use (for managing
projects, such as PRINCE2®, or P30 to manage
programmes of work, or COBOL to write code) has no
more than a passing influence on how many people are
needed in an organisation. More amusingly (or less,
depending on your tolerance levels) is the assumption that
business people will accept that recommendations made in
the name of ITIL® will have any credence (a fairly broad
clue as to why that should be lies in the letters IT ...... and,
come to that, infrastructure).

This is not to imply that ITIL® is not useful, or that it has
tremendous value, it is simply to reinforce that it is not, and
was not, a method or means written with the intent of
improving, or advising, about anything but the IT
infrastructure – any other interpretation is just that – an
interpretation with no official, or even unofficial,
endorsement. What seems very odd to many observers is
how and why the strength of a brand has been parlayed into
some form of omniscient guidance about any subject under
the sun.

So what silver bullets are available? Because the reason
people clutch at the ITIL® straw is the belief that somehow
all of the hard work has already been done, and a fully-
formed organisational change programme can be predicated
on some wise words from someone who has been down the

road before, and even better, it is credible, because it is in the name of ITIL®.

Sadly, the answer is there is no short cut. Accurate, organisational sizing can only be achieved through observation and measurement of work being performed. Further, the work being performed should be necessary (a surprising amount of the activity of a person may not be simply unproductive, it may be unnecessary). Processes should be efficient and people should have an appropriate workload. And when you know all of that, it is possible to look at interfaces and management hierarchies.

And this is not just to throw stones at ITIL®; IT is the problem – why would any business accept that organisational change would be the province of IT, when the majority of IT people clearly know little about the business? It is not simply the conceit that is laughable, but also the inability of IT to identify the blindingly obvious.

As always, if it looks too good to be true, then it certainly is … !

Necessary work

A key concept that everyone will recognise is that of necessary work. In strict terms of organisational change (in the domain of staff inspection and evaluation), this means establishing that the post (job), or (more accurately) all of the tasks/activities that comprise the post of a person, are germane. The issue of whether the activities are organised efficiently, or undertaken in a timely manner, is secondary at this point – as is the issue of the activities being commensurate with levels of responsibility (and ultimately pay grade).

Staff inspection on a regular basis ('regular' being a moveable feast but every five years – or when new working practices were introduced – was not uncommon in government departments) is considered necessary to ensure that the work performed by a person is necessary for the existence of the organisation. Over time, people drift into performing activities that are not necessary to the continued existence of the organisation (either because they are irrelevant, or processes have been created that are superfluous, or even because a person creates activities that, either through inefficient management, or lack of understanding, have come to be part of the routine) and some are simply inefficient.

The activities of a person should be:

- Necessary
- Well defined
- Properly understood
- Efficient
- Manageable
- Commensurate with responsibility
- Performed in a timely manner.

These elements apply irrespective of pay grade, industry sector, or, indeed, where a person sits in any organisation. Just about the only negotiable component of a post is 'thinking time' – some organisations view some posts as requiring time to resolve problems, or design solutions, and an allowance for these more ephemeral activities must be catered for. Many organisations will also dispense with the notion of a 'working day' for highly-paid executives, irrespective of employment laws worldwide. Directives, such as the EU 40 hour working week, can be applied at a certain level, but if anyone reading this seriously believes that the directive is adhered to by executives in any industry domain (including government), then it is likely they also believe in fairies!

It is not simply the expectation of an employer that makes the lip service to such directives so risible; it is the fact that people simply lie about adherence because they have work to do. An unnamed former colleague routinely worked 12-hour days and at least one day at the weekend, every week (including what he hilariously declared vacations), and in workload reporting, simply listed five eight-hour days.

Ironically, the issue of necessary versus unnecessary work will (almost) never be addressed in such circumstances. Another irony is that staff inspection and evaluation research established long ago that over three hours of an eight-hour working day for *any* individual is wholly unproductive (lunch breaks, personal time, interruptions) and, where staff are being assessed, this allowance is included in any calculation of time needed to carry out necessary work.

For most organisations, it is a major issue where a large workforce is employed, especially for clerical functions (e.g. insurance, banking); sadly, observation over a period (the longer the period and the more observations in that period using a range of staff) is the only means of arriving at calculations that are statistically correct.

Surprisingly, some people put their faith in computers to record working time and to ensure the veracity of input; they go to great lengths to identify tasks or categories against which a dutiful employee can make an entirely fictitious entry (see also EU Working Time Directive). The point here is that entering the time taken to perform a task is entirely different to the actual amount of time expended and could well be very different to the amount of time that should have been expended.

The only way to establish that necessary work is being carried out efficiently and competently is by observation.

The good news is that you can record your observations in your computer.

Numbers

So once the drudge of identifying and observing necessary work is being undertaken, how do you identify the number of people you need. Well, the first question should be how much work is there to do? If we take one of our ITIL® examples, the service desk, one question to answer would be how many calls arrive each day? Another would be how many e-mails? And after observation, you should have a good idea how long it takes to resolve these instances of work. You should also be able to arrive at identified inefficiencies, or perhaps areas where automation might help (rather than hinder), for example, call management software, or some form of software that creates records of reported calls/e-mails/visits.

You may also recommend working practices to improve overall performance at the expense of individual customer service; that may sound like a foolish thing to do, but what if a very helpful service desk analyst regularly spends an inordinate amount of time attempting to resolve issues faced by a caller? It might be that a script should be designed to 'walkthrough' a solution procedure, or a time limit identified, after which a call must be recorded and escalated to a specialist, or maybe a more comprehensive recommendation that solution scripts be made available to callers.

All impact on the time taken by an analyst and each will have a different impact on staff numbers. And don't forget to allow for personal time in any calculations, including the number of vacation days (see the next paragraph).

A more complex issue is that of supervision; generally speaking, a span of control of seven to one is optimum, according to staff inspection and evaluation research. That means, if you identify that seven people are needed to carry out the necessary work of your service desk, you will need one more person to supervise them. Seven is also considered to be a magic number in terms of planning for continuity/contingency. One more person is added to allow for vacation time, at least in the civilised countries of Europe, where vacation time generally exceeds four weeks. In certain third world countries, two weeks is considered generous and pregnant women are expected to work until the midwife is standing outside (and then they have to get back to work with the infant strapped to their backs).

Putting to one side the idiosyncratic nature of US healthcare, the point is that observation and measurement of actual work processes, together with analysis of workload, establishes raw numbers. After that, you still use mathematics, but it is possible to be more creative with the numbers.

If we take our example further and think of large-scale call centres, it is not unlikely that large numbers of clerks will be required. Let's assume, for tidy calculations, that:

- 70 people are needed

- And that 10 more are then added, to allow for vacations, and so on.

We now also require 80 divided by 7 managers/supervisors; we can round that to 12.

What about supervision of those people? Two senior managers/supervisors might be needed. This is not job creation; how will the organisation function without some form of supervision? The individuals tasked with supervisory work must also be assessed for efficiency; their job descriptions may well include escalated issues, dealing with difficult customers and staff reporting.

The point here is that until the component hierarchy has been assessed and built, the overall hierarchical organisation cannot be built. This is discussed later in this chapter.

Just to add to the labour intensive nature of this, consider also the need to look at business growth factors; your calculations must also be sufficiently robust to ensure that the organisational change of today lasts only until tomorrow. Business capacity management becomes important and a good IT capacity manager should be able to dig themselves out of technology for long enough to help with examination of business forecasts for growth. They might also be able to suggest ideas for using IT in the future to automate tasks efficiently.

Needs of the organisation

Figure 11 represents some of the needs that would be represented in almost any business. The needs of the owner, the employee (the actor), those regulating the business and

sector, the owner may also be representing the shareholders, and in the public sector, the customer is, of course, you and I.

How can these soft systems be instantiated using any method (IT or otherwise)? They usually end up in some form of hierarchical arrangement.

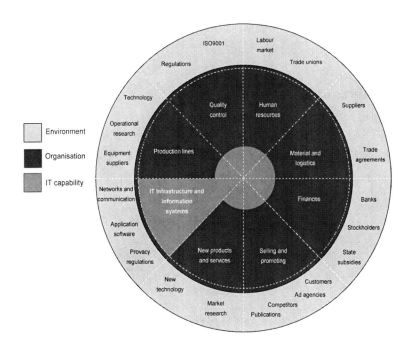

Figure 11: An unstructured organisation

Grading

Grading of staff is related to hierarchies, in terms of responsibility; it is also an issue for pay grading, though the relationship is complicated by other factors (that are the

relationship is complicated by other factors (that are the province of HR), such as commission, where appropriate, performance pay, shift pay, localisation, and many other factors. Changing the organisation will inevitably result in HR involvement (another factor that is often overlooked when a favourite 'method' is employed).

When it comes to executive grading and remuneration, even HR may take a back seat, since the Board of Directors, or other similar body, will likely set salary and package.

Hierarchies

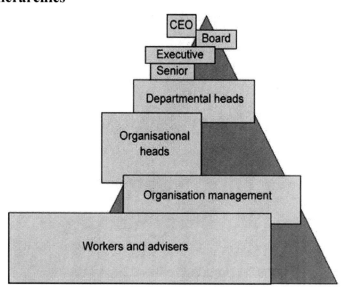

Figure 12: Traditional hierarchy

Hierarchies are, at best, a necessary evil; it is interesting that the typical pyramid hierarchy – Figure 12 – with CEO at the pinnacle and worker bees at the base, still exists, and

it is often amusing to see the way that so-called flat –
Figure 13 (or at least on the surface, flatter) organisations
have come to be seen as either more efficient, or perhaps
less divisive (get rid of the archaic class structures of the
capitalist bourgeoisie, and replace them with socio-anarchic
revolutionary Marxist structures, even though we are still
capitalist), or maybe even seen as enabling swifter and
more open communications between the person at the top
and the minions at the bottom (of course, all CEOs desire
that level of intimacy, do they not?).

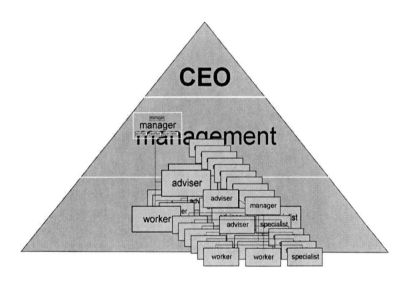

Figure 13: Flattened hierarchy

The reality is that flat structures often have labyrinthine
management hierarchies that become established very
quickly because, well, someone has to be the boss. And
someone has to report on how things are going. And
someone has to be responsible. And the boss does not have
time to deal with everyone, do they? And then we invent

'dotted lines' to represent matrices of management – because that is still better than those old-fashioned pyramids.

Many organisations are proud of their flat structure that goes from Executive to Senior Vice President, to Vice President to Director, to whoever does the work. Then when the structure is examined, it is discovered that some executives report to other executives, and some SVPs report to others – and then some VPs have many VPs working for them – all of these matrices being born from some perceived hierarchical need that the ancient and discredited pyramid structure could not possibly handle.

Putting aside such pre-conceptions, these internecine relationships create elaborate pay structures and reporting lines that are no more (or less) efficient than those the structure was created to replace. This is not a criticism of the need to manage, it is simply a reflection that management will always be enacted in some form of hierarchy.

They also create headaches where processes were not fully designed or thought through, to enable efficient work to be carried out. These structures were not created to facilitate efficient work processing; they were created to solve political problems, or to recreate the workflows that were a necessary part of a pyramidal hierarchy.

The nature of any management hierarchy must be to manage the efficient running of the processes necessary to ensure the survival of the business. Often the hierarchy simply evolves to manage what is considered important by individuals, as well as the needs of the business. Such evolutions are often the result of a perceived need, but are not engineered to be efficient, only expedient.

A good example would be the travel policy of a business; if an unscrupulous employee exploits the system, measures are often put in place to compensate. The measures may well solve the immediate problem, but create inefficiencies overall. Partly, this is because systems are believed to be more efficient than management, and partly because management inefficiency is rarely cited as the cause of knee-jerk reactions to problems.

Another good (or bad) example of a hierarchy that evolves is Communism. On the face of it, the organisation has been created to get rid of the imperialist capitalist bourgeoisie – see above – where everyone is important. But – because the collective needs to be managed, someone has to step forward to take responsibility. And then someone needs to be able to make sure that the instructions for the workers are carried out for the good of the collective, so lieutenants need to be appointed who can be trusted to carry out the will of the people (or to be precise, the person who stepped forward and rather likes the position of telling the people what their will actually is), and soon we have a hierarchy.

Of course, this is a democratic hierarchy that the collective can disagree with.

Not to labour the point, the issue is that the hierarchies do not always represent what is needed by the organisation, irrespective of domain (or government). Since hierarchies are unavoidable, an organisation should really consider how functions are best suited to the overall need and use process definition (discussed next) to establish common workflows within the functional hierarchy.

Process hierarchy

It has become fashionable to look at organisations from the process perspective because it is assumed that if we identify and define process flow(s), then it will be quickly apparent that management responsibilities will follow. Thus, if we define, say, the change management process, a change manager can be appointed and change staff – to do the work. Or perhaps the organisation thinks levels of service are most important to manage because someone stood up at a conference and told them so. Maybe they now want to create a team based on 'service levels to the business'. Some perceived notion of responsibility is then arbitrarily assigned and maybe a director is needed to manage the function, and then someone asks the *'How many people?'* question. And worse, the *'And what, precisely, will they be doing?'* And, perhaps worse than that, the *'How do we define change management?'* question.

Most often, organisations jump from one perceived 'method' of defining what to manage to another because it is assumed that one answer exists, and because the alternative – identifying what people do and how long it takes to do it, and if whatever they do can be made more efficient – is too much like hard work.

IT is a case in point; because it is actually quite difficult to be definitive about some of the work performed, it is assumed that it cannot be done – providing an excuse to change the organisation according to whim, or, more often, spurious interpretation of guidance that does not apply either to organisational change, or to managing organisations. That does not mean the guidance is not useful; it does mean, however, that changing the job title on the door of an individual to match the title of a guide to managing a process may not be the smartest idea in the world.

One reason that many organisations have embraced process guidance is that management silos have created boundaries over many years that hinder effective management. Proponents of managing with the guidance of a process hierarchy argue that the all-embracing nature of a manager who is responsible for managing, say, IT change, or perhaps levels of service, or IT configuration, will break down those established silos. The reality, however, is that silos of a different nature are created, and boundaries that create other problems.

Some of the reasons for the failure of the process management approach are:

- The scope of the process was not clearly identified.
- The process was not understood and not defined clearly.
- Interfaces between, and responsibilities of, process managers, were often unclear and conflicting.
- The cultural change required to alter an IT centric organisation into a customer service centric organisation was not addressed.
- Resistance to change was not addressed.

And just to throw in another point, if the IT organisation was not being managed effectively, why would a redefinition of a process alter that?

Changing the effectiveness of management requires a fundamental change in culture, attitude and behaviour.

Using process roles

More useful than identifying process managers, is allocating responsibility for a process (or more than one process, depending on the needs/workload analysis) to other managerial responsibilities. This is not to say that large organisations should never create management roles, based on, for example, managing IT change or managing incidents; such decisions should always be based on the amount of necessary work that an individual can reasonably perform, weighed against the amount of work that has to be done.

The use of roles does not eliminate the need to address cultural and behavioural issues. Indeed, it remains fundamental to changing established patterns that have led to the need to address organisational change.

Behavioural change can be brought about through:

- Training
- Persuasion
- Reward
- Sanction.

Sanction is often a last resort and, where individuals simply refuse to conform to new or expected patterns of behaviour, it cannot be ignored. Another reason for failure to change an organisation is that changes in behaviour are not linked to HR systems.

If your organisation is spending many thousands on training and education, but there is no redress for the recalcitrant, then the money is wasted. Reward good behaviour and address bad behaviour.

CHAPTER 6: USING IT TO CATALYSE BUSINESS TRANSFORMATIONS

Introduction

This chapter revisits our introductory themes, and amplifies some of the points we made there in regard to the symbiotic (some would argue parasitic) link between business and IT. IS and IT may be painful to control and manage, and the long-standing belief that it is both expensive and under-performing, not to say unresponsive, often leads to IT being relegated to a subsidiary role, as we discussed, being engaged very late in strategic planning. The role of IT capabilities and deployment in making the transformations should not be underestimated.

Merger or acquisition

If, for example, your organisation is to be taken over, responsibility for the future of IT support to your business may be in the hands of the new owner. However, you will still need to think about business continuity to make sure that IT support to your business continues to be provided and managed during any transition period. The change facing 'your IT' might be a simple handover to new management, or it might be a much riskier move to equivalent IT systems already used by the new owners. Here, IT may well be considered to be a pain, but the situation can be turned to the advantage of both parties by thinking about new capabilities and business transformations that could be planned as part of the organisational changes that will inevitably follow.

Most often, merging businesses will involve merging IT providers (internal, external or a combination!). A useful checklist when in the merger/acquisition position follows:

- Is information provided accurately and on time?
- How many databases are in use in each business?
- Are the businesses content with their provider?
- How much does IT cost?
- Is IT perceived as poor value?
- How long does it take to develop new systems?
- Are they delivered on time, to budget, and are they reliable?
- Which IT organisation's services are provided and used in the most coherent way?
- Which has a fragmented approach to applications and technology?
- What cultural differences will need to be resolved?
- Does one provider work to recognised standards and methods, such as IS020000, ISO27001, PRINCE2®, and so on?
- Are there different skill sets?
- Will different technologies combine harmoniously?
- Is there a need for a single set of applications and a single technology platform – if so, how will it be achieved?
- What is the cost of parallel running of the IT organisations?
- Are the business processes different?
- Must they be rationalised – when and how?
- Are pay structures different – is this a problem?
- What is the strategic direction of the businesses?
- How are projects involving radical change managed now and will this change?

- Which business will need to adapt its IT most, e.g. to match strategic direction?
- Can IT expenditure be saved – where and how?
- Which business processes could be the focus for IT effort to deliver maximum value to the merged businesses?
- Which business skills must be developed by the new, merged IT function?
- Which IT skills should be developed by the business to create a true partnership with IT?
- Is a central IT function needed? Should it be organised to reflect the needs of the businesses?

Don't forget to justify any proposals with a business case! Mergers and acquisitions are such an important consideration to change in modern times, that a separate appendix (Appendix 1) is included, with more discussions.

Defining requirements

To assist with making changes to the organisation as smooth as possible, you should try to define requirements and user acceptance criteria (what functions and operational issues a new service must satisfy, in order to be accepted by the business for operational use) by using one or more of the following:

- Business or business models
- Business threads
- Existing user procedures manuals
- System boundary definitions
- User task scenarios.

Business models

You can build a model of business activities after the change (or at least after the new IT application is delivered) which is not information system oriented. For example, you can use a soft systems approach to define the business processes that satisfy business goals, define monitoring, feedback and control mechanisms for these processes, and define processes to resolve conflicting goals.

Business threads

As part of the business or business model you can define what may be called 'business threads' which describe your key business processes, by following a case from its beginning to end. A business thread may take weeks or months to complete and ends in a payment, or other business objective.

Existing user procedure manuals

These are useful, provided that they actually represent what people do (very often they do not) and provided that they, or the new IT applications, will continue to do so after the new IT application is delivered.

System boundary definitions

From the documents described, you can define the boundary of an information system (or various possible information systems) needed to support the business activities, business threads and user procedures.

User task scenarios

Having defined a system boundary, you can define what may be called user task scenarios, which are the activities that a user will be expected to undertake in some form of short-term dialogue with the information system. One of the best ways to do this is by means of specific examples, which can be used as test cases in system testing and user acceptance testing.

Changing business capabilities

Every organisation will need new, or altered, IT capabilities, and to deploy IT differently as time goes on; as legislation is created; as mergers and acquisitions take place … the list goes on. You can use the conceptual model given in Figure 14 (first discussed in Chapter 1) and take a before-and-after perspective to help you to scope the areas of the business that are going to be changed. That will help to focus your attention on where the IT capabilities and IT deployment of the business may have to change. However, before you go too far down that track, you should link back to the business capabilities you will need and how much they will have to change from what you have now.

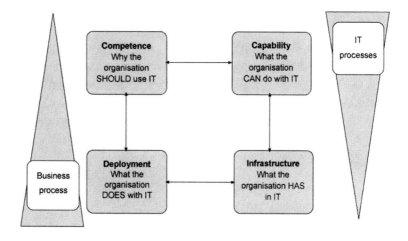

Figure 14: A business perspective on IT

The business capabilities that a change is intended to create, or alter, should be clear from the motivation for the change, or, if not, it should, at least, be possible to identify the capability changes needed. You can again use the conceptual model in Figure 14 to help you to scope the changes. You may need professional help to carry out business analyses in order to fully identify the changes in business capabilities that you will need.

At this stage incidentally, you should be concentrating on business added value capabilities. If you have an IT service catalogue, you will know which IT services provide the IT capabilities; if you have a software inventory, you will know which IT applications provide the capabilities. Unless you are unlucky, you should find that there is a simple mapping between business capabilities and IT applications (unless you are very lucky, you will not find it so easy to map these to IT devices and networks!). If the information linking business capabilities to IT services and applications is not readily available, and if there isn't a simple mapping, you will have to call in your internal IT experts, or outside consultants, to get this information.

For those business capabilities that do not have to change as a result of the proposals, you will be able to form an initial assessment of the IT applications that are likely to remain unchanged. From a knowledge of the business capabilities that are no longer needed, you will be able to deduce which IT applications are unlikely to be needed in the future. That leaves the trickier problem of new, or altered, business capabilities, that may need new, or altered, IT capabilities, which may, in turn, mean modifying existing IT applications, or developing, or acquiring, new applications (the various options for modification were discussed in Chapter 3).

It isn't just IT applications that are designed to support particular business functions that you should consider. You also need to consider general purpose IT capabilities, such as e-mail, that you may already have, to assess whether you will still need them in the same way, and, if so, whether they need to be improved or modified – or sourced from the Cloud … For example, you may want your electronic mail system to be accessible to third-party personnel, who are either out on the road, or working from home. You may also need new generic IT capabilities, such as video conferencing at the desktop. E-mail is so ubiquitous that it is often overlooked as something that has been around for a long time; the fact is that it may still be a source for innovation and part of organisational change.

Sharing and integrating computerised information (to make information sharing easier within the business) is probably the single most important business capability/issue that IT should be facilitating. Often misconstrued as knowledge management, information sharing is a cornerstone of knowledge management and can be a driver for transforming the organisation

To make the change effective, you may need to increase the deployment of IT in support of particular business areas or support functions, such as personnel, development/management or marketing – or maybe all of these.

Opportunity

Now is the time to think about rectifying other problems with your existing IT capabilities. For example, if you know you will run out of IT capacity in six months, you should make sure a capacity upgrade is included in your requirements for IT change to support the business change. Neither the business nor the IT organisations should require alteration resulting from technology upgrades, though appropriate training to specific areas will be needed.

As another example, if you are dissatisfied with the control you have over your IT infrastructure, you should think about improving management as one of your IT change requirements. If you are locked in to a legacy application that no one dares change, which is actually stifling business improvement, now might be the time to take decisive action.

You should distinguish between wants and needs. If you 'need' certain new, or altered, IT capabilities to enable the rapid change, the chances are that you will need them from day one of the new business operation, so these changes must get priority. You may even need some of the capability during the change itself. You must be clear about what is needed when. If you only 'want' other changes to IT capabilities, maybe you can make do without them for a while, to give yourself more time to make the urgent changes work.

However, you must know where your IT is heading, if you are to harness it and make it play a full and successful part in the ongoing effectiveness of your business. Each successive change should be a step on the way to your IT of the future, not an advance down a blind alley.

Future proofing

You need to make sure your IS/IT planners have a target architecture for the IT applications and IT infrastructure to which they are working. New applications and new infrastructure should, wherever possible, be architecture-conformant, with the objectives of making it easy to:

- Change the portfolio of applications without having to change the underlying technology.
- Change the underlying technology without having to change the applications.
- Facilitate the interworking of applications and the sharing of data across the IT infrastructure and across the business, perhaps also with the partners of the business.

In times of radical change

A fundamental issue for business managers to consider in times of radical change is that organisational characteristics and information sources will be relatively unstable;

fluctuating with changing conditions and as thinking evolves – perhaps even as new technology is acquired.

However, many of the core business processes and the underlying data are likely to be relatively stable, and once they are properly understood, the organisational characteristics and IT needed to conduct those aspects of the business become apparent. The most significant improvements are often made through examination and re-engineering of the business processes and data repositories, rather than through the restructuring of the business's organisation and information flows.

Fundamental changes require lots of time, people, patience, cold towels, money, food and water. In times of change, time is often the component in shortest supply. Go for early, demonstrable wins, and easy targets. Introduce change progressively, concentrating on high-priority aspects.

Obtain blueprints for the new IT infrastructure

Unless your needs for new, or altered, IT capabilities result in simple and straightforward changes to the IT infrastructure, you will probably find it helpful to get your IT planners to formulate a series of blueprints for the IT infrastructure. These blueprints will cover the major milestones in the transformation of the IT infrastructure, from supporting the pre-change business, through the change itself, into 'what we must have' to bring the change into operation, through to a steady state in which the IT infrastructure is brought into an optimised state for the new business and developed as the new business needs evolve.

CHAPTER 7: SUMMARY OF MAIN ISSUES

Introduction

Although discussed extensively in this book, IT will be mentioned only in the later paragraphs in this chapter. The reason being (as was mentioned in the Preface and stressed throughout the book) that IT should follow business change!

From experience of being involved with numerous IT-related business change projects (and many projects for business transformation that were *not* predicated on use of IT), in both the public and private sectors, we have drawn together key, often common, elements that need to be addressed when managing change. The following guidance arises from that experience; keep in mind that as we have mentioned several times, managing organisational change is not appropriate to cookie-cutter guidance. The points summarised in this section are useful as guidance, but are not definitive or mandatory.

Summary of key issues

The following is a list of issues and possible solutions that arise irrespective of organisation type, or country of operation, or market sector:

- Signal change from the top: the Board/Executive must show it means business and is committed to a successful outcome.
- Use a formal approach to document and communicate the business position: obtain a

thorough understanding of business direction and provide top down mapping of business processes at the outset, leading to a clear statement of business vision (mission, goals, future investment, etc.).

- Articulate the consequences: be clear what the consequences of non action will be. Use quotes from key members of the Board and staff, for example, mentioning the demands of central government legislators, or from shareholders; discussing the imperatives for cutting costs perhaps, or even for survival of the business.

- Develop a full and shared understanding of the environment and capabilities: consider stakeholder interests (HM Treasury – perhaps if you work within UK government, the General Accounts Office (GAO) in the USA, or shareholders in private sector companies), market needs (customer requirements, new products, new sales channels), the competition, staff capabilities, capacity for change. This understanding needs to be shared at board level, with members giving their commitment.

- Define and endorse an 'operating vision': what is needed to take the business into the next century – a vision that satisfies aspirations, meets customer needs, and satisfies HM Treasury, or shareholders.

The operating vision

Capturing a vision that will resonate is fraught; far too often it seems to be nothing more than corporate Marxism, particularly when employees can easily recognise slogans that are being reused from other organisations.

Sloganeering most often leads to a genuine disdain for the corporate body that may lead to employee apathy; particularly unfortunate given that the vision is intended to improve relations and corporate focus. Lip service becomes common, but true adoption remains absent.

Consultation is an excellent approach, engaging employees in the process; managing expectations of the employees within the process is much harder. Continuous feedback on why some things are taken on board, and why others are not, is very important.

Try to capture the vision in a number of goals or critical success factors which can be used as a focus for change.

Examples could be:

- Customer focused processing
- Organisational flexibility
- Integration of alternative sales channels
- Reduced operating costs
- Job design to facilitate empowerment and a highly-motivated workforce
- Integration of management information requirements.

It is difficult to get the right mission statement; the need to achieve buy-in means that inevitably compromise will result. This can mean that the mission is watered down substantially; resist this, because you need a clear focus for change and improvement.

Identifying the core business is never easy. For example, you may be very focused on supporting areas which are close to the business centre, even if these are not critical in delivering the main business goals. This kind of mismatch can result in conflicts.

Step change is sometimes necessary to achieve the goals set. The business may need a step change if its goals are to be achieved. This drives the next step – the identification of a necessary transformation strategy.

Strategy for the transformation

Use a project to achieve the strategy. Setting up a project transformation to identify the appropriate strategy ensures that a strategy is identified and agreed. The scoping study should have clearly-defined and tangible goals, all within a defined timescale.

Motivating any business, especially in the public sector where multiple programmes co-exist or even conflict, to pull together project teams, takes time. There is a need to balance continuity with freshness, but changes (particularly if posts needed to manage projects need to be advertised before being filled) take time.

Facilitation and enabling ensures client ownership. Because a strategy is such a key component in ensuring future success, it is essential to get ownership of the findings. This can be achieved by assuming a facilitative style of leadership during this phase. You might have to buy in facilitation skills.

Involve many people at this stage to ensure commitment. Because the vision and emerging strategy are well known to the project team, there is a tendency to be complacent on communications. Lack of communication at this stage simply creates an environment where resistance is common and problems for the future are left to fester (or should that be mature?).

Balanced objectives for the transformation help sell the concept that the critical success factors need to be well balanced. There should be benefits for stakeholders, staff, customers and management. This helps to sell the concept to decision makers.

Agenda for the transformation

You need to move quickly from mapping, to other transformation mediums, to aid understanding. Mapping is excellent for understanding and re-engineering processes. However, there is a need to move quickly to other methods which support IT requirements – programme planning, risk management, project planning and process/procedure preparation.

Cartoons aid communications. This is a serious comment. Large-size cartoons can be prepared which show staff how the new processes are to operate. These can be an excellent tool for communication at all levels of the business, particularly if you intend becoming more customer facing.

An end objective is necessary for planning the agenda. As the workload increases, it is important to be clear with the team where work is leading.

It is easy to underestimate the implementation resources required, because work to this point will most probably have taken place within small teams. It is also easy to underestimate the effort required in later stages.

Execute the transformation

Communications become harder and more important at this stage. During the implementation phases of an IT programme, the workloads increase considerably. It is not possible to get all those involved with the programme together regularly, or sometimes, at all. There is a need to communicate progress to a wider audience.

It is difficult to choose between implementing projects first, or choosing the right people first. Do you choose the projects to suit the people available, or try to find people to fit the projects?

Get the implementation structure right. There are a number of ways to organise the effort – these might need to change as the transformation progresses. Launch the programme first. Individual projects seldom deliver transformation objectives. It is critical to maintain elements, such as the vision and programme approach, during this stage.

It takes time to change. Transformation in a large business is often only achievable over a period of several years.

It takes considerable and careful planning. Because of the extent of change, considerable work needs to be done up front – proving the concept, establishing the business case, preparing for new systems, co-ordinating change timings, etc.

Strong leadership is essential. The extent of inertia and resistance to change in a large business is almost overwhelming. Strong leadership is essential to create momentum and maintain the coherence of the programme.

There are substantial risks when the business comes on board; when the business gets behind the programme, the risks change. The worst danger becomes derailment, as people try to take the programme in different directions – according to their political persuasion and personal involvement. The programme management style needs to be a combination of both strict and flexible – to keep control, yet also to encourage participation.

Skills are required that don't necessarily exist in the business or in IT. A large programme of change, and the extent of the changes that are needed, often puts great strain on the people in the business organisation. Skills needed for managing projects, radically changing personnel structures and terms and conditions, and transforming business processes, need to be imported or developed through training. Of course, the same is true of IT, and here the business may need to take a leading role in ensuring that critical IT skills are in place. The risk in not having the skills is to the business; IT service provision will be impacted and though IT may be blamed for failures, it is the business that suffers.

Programme and project management

The fundamental rule in good programme management is to make sure that each project in a change programme has clear objectives, with roles and responsibilities defined unambiguously. The required outputs from the project (such as a new IT application, or trained users) must be specified precisely, to allow proper assessment of when (or if …) they have been delivered, and whether they are acceptable. The project planning process will indicate not only when the outputs can be delivered, staged if necessary, but also the resources needed to deliver them. Project estimating is by no means an exact science, but good managers can certainly learn to get better at it through practice.

It will pay dividends to focus particular attention on contracts where IT, or portions of IT, are outsourced (or perhaps where the changes involve the outsourcing of any current in-house IT service). If you are relying on third parties, it is essential that you are protected by your contract with them. Who will pay penalties if, for example, applications are not built and tested in time for implementation? What are the consequences of having to revert to the original IT infrastructure, if there is a failure in installing a new one? Indeed, who is responsible for developing and testing business continuity plans to be invoked when crises occur? A sensible rule is to let nothing 'fall down the cracks'. If it is important to you, someone must take responsibility for its ongoing successful operation.

IT skills

The IT business unit may not have enough people of the right calibre to cope with the changes, help with organisational change, maintain provision of services, and to keep IT support running smoothly. It pays to be realistic about this. IT is probably far too important to the organisation to be squeezed into available manpower.

If there is time, it might be possible to grow the internal IT skills, so as to increase the number of people you can call on to cope with IT during change. It is more likely that there will not be time, or you won't feel it is cost-justifiable to meet what is, after all, a short-term requirement. The longer-term issue of new skills will be a different issue.

In the short term, to cope with change, it is possible you will have to call on contractors. You may want to use such outside help to top up internal expertise in areas that are important in a time of radical business change, for example:

- IS architectures
- IT infrastructure planning
- Specification of requirements (for software to support the business)
- Management of risk
- Data, design and database experts
- Networks expertise
- Project management
- Software development
- System integration
- Testing of software and systems
- IT transition planning and management
- Strategies for legacy systems.

Also, or alternatively, you may use outsiders to keep your IT systems going while you deploy your existing people on the planning, acquisition and implementation of the new IT infrastructure.

In either case, you will need to be assured of the long-term viability of the skills of the people in IT in each of the areas listed, or, in the case of outsourced IT, have access to some audit of the skills present in the provider organisation.

APPENDIX 1: MERGERS AND ACQUISITIONS

Introduction

Tyson Faulkner and Ed Furilla are deeply involved with acquisitions and mergers, and have been for many years. They were asked to provide their thoughts about the good practices they have identified that can be shared, and their perspective on organisational change. Why include a separate appendix about mergers and acquisitions? Well, one reason would be that organisational change is now going to affect two organisations and, in this case, a problem halved is not a problem solved; in fact, the problem is more than doubled. Two groups of people, one group almost certainly feeling vulnerable; two cultures most likely; two sets of processes to think about, and of course, two IT organisations. Thus, it is worth spending a few moments thinking of this as an intriguing set of circumstances.

Throughout this appendix, when we refer to an acquisition we are referring to the term 'Mergers and Acquisitions' (M&A). To a lesser degree, we include divestitures in this concept; however, there are differences that apply to a divestiture that we will not cover, either here or elsewhere, in this book.

Let's begin by setting the context (or the life cycle) of an acquisition. The acquisition life cycle begins with an overall business strategy which answers questions, such as:

- Should we be making an acquisition or building the capability organically?
- What type of acquisition is required?

- What is the business plan for an acquisition (revenue targets, purchase price, etc.)?

These questions not only kick off the process of selection, but are carried out throughout the entire process to ensure value is identified from the outset, as well as being monitored once the target company is fully integrated. Figure 15 outlines the major components found in the life cycle.

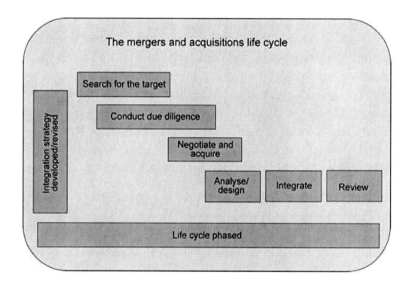

Figure 15: The M&A life cycle

Within the phases of the life cycle, a decision will be made regarding the integration strategy to be adopted. This decision typically follows the due diligence phase and is factored into the design phase. Figure 16 outlines the four principal types of strategies that are assessed for possible adoption; they include: Co-existence, Absorption, Best-of-Breed, and Transformation.

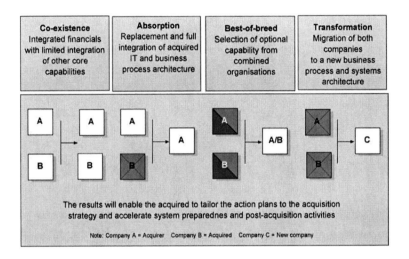

Figure 16: Strategies

Based on the size of the acquisitions performed, typically smaller companies being the prey of larger, there is a tendency to assume most will be small scale (that is the Absorption type); however, even then it is not uncommon to find companies preferring 'Co-existence' as the integration strategy. Such decisions are based on business rationale for that specific acquisition and the ability of the business to minimise the potential business interruption of the target company. As the size of an acquisition increases (i.e. more of a 'merger of equals'), or unique systems and processes are identified, 'Best-of-Breed' would more likely come into play. Transformation is typically not an alternative that is used, due to the radical change required and the likelihood that neither company's systems and processes would satisfy the needs of the combined companies.

Acquisitions

Acquisitions are often used as a means of developing, or enhancing, a company's product and/or services strategy. This approach is typically used to:

- Speed up the time required to enter into a specific market
- Obtain a new line of revenue
- Augment the existing portfolio of products
- Obtain unique service skills and capabilities.

These strategies can range from increasing market share, growth in a particular market segment, or entering into new markets, to name just a few. Since a target company's people are often the asset being procured, the need for understanding and effectively managing the organisational change, often comes to the fore more rapidly than was planned. People in this position feel vulnerable because the history of acquisitions is not one that lends to a feeling of security.

Many companies have worked to establish a set of integration tools and methods that look at an acquisition from the three separate and distinct perspectives that we have been discussing throughout this book: people, process and technology. These elements are viewed slightly differently when people, process and technology are related to an acquisition.

The most significant factor in any acquisition is people (despite IT thinking that we all exist to serve IT). The most notable feature is the culture of the target company – is it in alignment with the culture of the acquiring company? Take another look at the political perspectives discussion in Chapter 3 and discussions about dominant characteristics of an organisation in Chapter 4. Organisational culture can best be thought of as the pattern of actions, words, beliefs and behaviours, that members of a business organisation share (hence our earlier discussions about politics and characteristics). This is also sometimes referred to as the DNA of the organisation. As an acquired company is brought into the acquiring company, there is an increased attention to understanding the culture, or DNA, as it relates to the overall change initiative.

Process alignment

The next aspect of focus is in the area of business process alignment. Here we look at the organisation from the perspective of the business, to determine where there may be gaps and/or overlaps. For example, many processes adopted by one company, while they may look the same, are very different than those of another, in terms of how they are enacted or proceduralised. Sometimes, seemingly simple changes can create a significant dissatisfaction to either the employees, or worse, to the customers of the acquired company. Employees and their customers are comfortable dealing with (business) processes in a specific manner. When changes to the way they operate are made, even when those changes are 'better', the potential for dissatisfaction exists. This is not to suggest that we avoid making those changes, but more to indicate that we should fully understand the difference and ensure that we take those differences into account before making changes. In addition, by understanding the differences, we can create a communications strategy that will help reduce the chance of negative perceptions being developed.

Technology

The technology component deals with the infrastructure and applications aspects of the integration process. Under the infrastructure, we typically look at integrating networks, servers, mail and messaging, etc. Application integration focuses on both the data and business information systems. This is further divided into two parts: front-office and back-office. From the back-office perspective, the key goals are usually centered on reduced operating costs and/or increasing control. Thus, issues, such as centralisation and shared services, often come into focus, and functions, such as finance, accounting, HR and procurement, are included. For front-office, or customer-facing systems, the objectives are more typically focused on increasing market share, improving the customer experience, and ensuring the behaviour of sales personnel is in alignment with the objectives of the acquisition.

Acquisitions continue to be a key business strategy for many companies. Therefore, acquisition integration processes have matured considerably over the past several years. This maturation has facilitated both the speed and the quality of the overall integration process. Improving the speed of integration enables the acceleration of time to value from the acquisition, while improvements to the overall quality of an integration result in enhanced employee and customer satisfaction – or at least, that is the theory! These improvements are enabled by assessing the people, process and technology areas mentioned above.

During the due diligence phase of the life cycle of an acquisition, an assessment should be performed by looking at the people, process and technology landscape of the target company. In addition, there should be a similar assessment of the acquiring company. It is recommended that an objective look at both companies is conducted, to ensure a full understanding of the impact of the acquisition is gathered. It is important to note that these processes will be used when needed and not necessarily be used in their full form for all acquisitions. For example, if the target is a small, 10 person software services company, we would recommend going through an assessment with much less rigour than for a 500 person product company. The steps will be the same, but the level of detail will be much less.

People

It has been claimed that many acquisitions seem to destroy shareholder value, rather than create it. This is not necessarily because the purchase price seems high, or because strategic fit seems to have been overlooked. Most often, the reason is that companies fail to win the support of customers and employees immediately after the merger – and that leads to problems. Understanding the different culture of each organisation is crucial to being able to successfully, and rapidly, blend the companies and their employees together, so that productivity and customer service are uninterrupted. In the same way that two people with wildly differing values and beliefs will not last long together as a couple, this is also true for organisations. Many companies include some form of cultural assessment as part of their due diligence process; many of course, do not.

A good approach is to survey a stratified, random sampling of each company's employees and to then compare the fit. Key factors to consider when assessing cultural fit are:

- Customer orientation
- Company philosophy
- Risk orientation
- Existing work/life balance
- Desired work/life balance
- Openness to diversity
- Experience with/openness to change
- How are messages communicated?
- Individualism
- Formality of hierarchy
- Decision-making process
- Job orientation
- Hiring practices
- Promotion practices
- Management philosophy
- Employee value proposition
- Employee attrition
- Performance management.

Figure 17 provides an example of what you can use to establish the importance of expected behaviours.

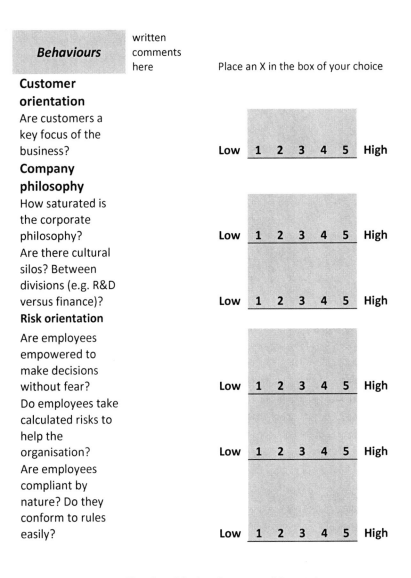

Figure 17: Matrix of behaviours and importance

As a result of an assessment, you are able to determine where there may be issues or obstacles related to the acquisition. And what do you do about that? Well, don't just make decisions based on the current policy, understand the implications of the decisions first and adjust according to the risks associated with this change.

Process

Business processes are the foundation for how the business will operate. It is critical to understand the processes of the target company and to compare them to those of the acquiring company. This will enable you to identify gaps and overlaps which will be used to understand and manage those processes. Without this understanding, the negative impact to the operating costs, employee and customer satisfaction, will not be understood.

The first step is to make a list of all business (and IT) processes by function, and then to determine which processes are deemed as high, medium or low priority. The priorities are established by the subject matter experts within the function, but may include input from other functions that are either upstream or downstream from that process. In addition to creating this inventory, the applications associated with each process should be established. We then need to map the processes of the target company to those of the acquiring company, to ensure we are comparing apples to apples. Figure 18 outlines an example of a learning management area and identifies a few processes associated with this function, the relative priority and the associated applications for that process. This will be used to further explore the processes to determine the ultimate disposition of that process.

PROCESSES	PRIORITY	ASSOCIATED APPLICATIONS
Education opportunity management/contracts order	1	SFDC/SAP (contracts)
Customer education registration/billing management	1	LMS, SAP (US), TOPS, ACD (call centre switch)
Education fulfilment/delivery	2	LMS, Surgient, Exam builder, Prometric, eval.com
Customer education resource management	3	Clarity, SharePoint, SAP C-Projects, VIPER

Figure 18: Associating applications and services

Once the priority process areas have been identified, it is recommended that a facilitated self-assessment be performed. The facilitated self-assessment should be attended by no less than three, ideally around five, employees, who execute the process being evaluated on a day-to-day basis. It is best facilitated by two individuals, one to drive the discussion, to ensure that the appropriate questions are answered to their fullest, and the other to focus on recording the results during the meeting. In other words, a trained facilitator guides the meeting, and another individual records the activity, and although this is more of a guideline, the meetings typically last 90 minutes. Less time doesn't allow for enough dialogue to collect the needed information and longer periods tend to cause people to lose interest in the discussion. If there is more time required, we recommend breaking down the process discussions into manageable pieces. Each facilitated session should be no more than 90 minutes.

During the meeting, it is important to define the process to ensure that everyone understands the points to be addressed. This high-level scoping exercise is crucial to ensure everyone is 'on the same page' regarding the boundaries, where the process start and ends. After the scoping step there are a set of questions related to the process. The initial questions collect some high-level information related to the process being addressed. They include questions related to process effectiveness and efficiency, process maturity and process scalability (i.e. can the process scale up to handle greater volumes?).

The information that is collected includes basic information related to any process. The type of information collected includes process owner, business area, geographical span, core systems/applications. This enables comparisons to be matched to similar processes running at the acquiring company.

The next set of information is to collect deals with more specific attributes related to the process being reviewed. This area should address the maturity of the process using an industry standard process maturity scale, as well as the overall quality, which asks questions dealing with process defects and the constraints related to process scalability. For example, a company that manages change efficiently will have a difficult transition to one where change is chaotic. Cultural issues, such as the management style of process adherence, will also be of interest. When Japanese companies began operations outside of Japan, creating subsidiary companies in the UK, for example, local personnel effectively had to be trained to understand Japanese culture. If a Japanese company acquires a western company, the absorption would require similar attention – training, persuasion, education – almost to the extent of enforcement; in order for business to be transacted in the same way.

Process efficiency and effectiveness are measured by comparisons to benchmark, overall timeliness of the process, process quality, customer satisfaction and cost. Essentially, you are trying to determine if the process is achieving the desired results. Once this is completed, there should be scoring of those results.

Maturity and scalability

Under the heading of maturity and scalability we look at the design, documentation, skills and ownership of the process, measures and controls. This allows you to determine how reliable the process is, and to determine if there are control weaknesses that would prohibit adoption of the process.

Once all the data is collected, there is a discussion that summarises the findings. Here we recommend using a SWOT analysis (Strengths, Weaknesses, Opportunities and Threats). This is possibly the most important step in the overall assessment process. It enables the team to outline the good, the bad and the ugly of a particular process. If facilitated properly, the group will be open and honest with the feedback provided and the end result will be an in-depth review of the process. This provides visibility into those areas which could be easy or difficult to implement. Expected changes ... Obviously this won't provide the answer, but it will establish a direction that can be pursued.

Technology

The next major area of focus deals with the acquired company's infrastructure and applications portfolio. The infrastructure area focuses on networks, data centres, electronic mail, storage and other aspects of running the business from an information technology perspective. The applications portfolio addresses information systems and data that supports the business, such as ERP, information data marts/warehousing, sales and sales operations systems, to name a few.

Each of these applications requires a detailed assessment to compare with the acquiring company's application portfolio and roadmap. This activity becomes especially critical for a large acquisition, or when a company is purchased that may have more robust solutions in a given area of the business.

This is typically managed by the IT personnel. Business systems (or enterprise) architects would perform this assessment. The assessment is generally performed by reviewing several aspects of the information technology platform. In order to structure the process, a series of questions are developed with a specific focus on the following areas:

- Application assessment
- Supportability risk
- Complexity and change sensitivity risk
- Architecture risk
- Database risk
- Operational risk
- Controls risk
- Security risk
- Application direction indicator

Appendix 1: Mergers and Acquisitions

- Information risk assessment
- Customer
- Product
- Finance
- Vendor
- HR
- Infrastructure assessment
- Technology domain (e.g. client platform, server, etc.)
- Business criticality
- Technology owner
- Technology in use (vendor, product, and version)
- Vendor supported?
- Vendor product status (e.g. generally available)
- Deployment status (e.g. standard, pilot)
- Instances deployed
- Managed by
- Support staff expertise (number, skill level)
- Information technology security assessment
- Logging
- Identity
- Authentication
- Access control
- Documentation
- Network security
- Security awareness
- Physical security
- Confidentiality and compliance
- Security organisation
- Platform security.

Once all the information is collected, it can be synthesised in a way to graphically represent the overall risk associated with a particular technology dimension.

Figure 19 provides an example of an application risk scorecard which establishes focus areas for a subsequent review.

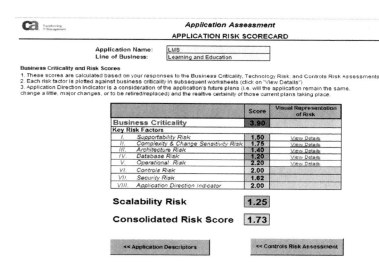

Figure 19: Application assessment

Summary

By and large, this approach provides for an objective view of the target company's 'people, process and technology' environments, as compared to the acquiring company's environments. It takes a fact-based approach and, where judgments have been applied, ensures the assumptions and the judgments these are based on are well known. Its comprehensive design provides a comprehensive, multi-dimensional view of each business area, through a quick and relatively simple to deploy set of methods and processes. The methods used can be adapted to focus on particular areas of interest, or to align to specific business strategies. Results can be weighted and the measurement system itself can be tailored to specific business standards; all of which allow for deep or shallow assessments. And it should be emphasised that the use of facilitated self-assessment, in conjunction with subject matter experts, is more effective than blind surveying, because it reveals differences of opinion. Collaboration also quickly resolves gaps through immediate knowledge transfer and, where judgment instead of data was used, helps to ensure consistency in responses.

ITG RESOURCES

IT Governance Ltd sources, creates and delivers products and services to meet the real-world, evolving IT governance needs of today's organisations, directors, managers and practitioners. The ITG website (*www.itgovernance.co.uk*) is the international one-stop-shop for corporate and IT governance information, advice, guidance, books, tools, training and consultancy.

Other Websites

Books and tools published by IT Governance Publishing (ITGP) are available from all Business booksellers and are also immediately available from the following websites:

www.itgovernance.co.uk/catalog/355 provides information and online purchasing facilities for every currently available book published by ITGP.

www.itgovernance.eu is our euro denominated website which ships from Benelux and has a growing range of books in European languages other than English.

www.itgovernanceusa.com is a US$-based website that delivers the full range of IT Governance products to North America, and ships from within the continental US.

www.itgovernanceasia.com provides a selected range of ITGP products specifically for customers in South Asia.

www.27001.com is the IT Governance Ltd website that deals specifically with information security management, and ships from within the continental US.

Pocket Guides

For full details of the entire range of pocket guides, simply follow the links at *www.itgovernance.co.uk/publishing.aspx*.

Toolkits

ITG's unique range of toolkits includes the IT Governance Framework Toolkit, which contains all the tools and guidance that you will need in order to develop and implement an appropriate IT governance framework for your organisation. Full details can be found at *www.itgovernance.co.uk/products/519*.

For a free paper on how to use the proprietary Calder-Moir IT Governance Framework, and for a free trial version of the toolkit, see *www.itgovernance.co.uk/calder_moir.aspx*.

There is also a wide range of toolkits to simplify implementation of management systems, such as an ISO/IEC 27001 ISMS or a BS25999 BCMS, and these can all be viewed and purchased online at: *www.itgovernance.co.uk/catalog/1*.

Best Practice Reports

ITG's range of Best Practice Reports is now at *www.itgovernance.co.uk/best-practice-reports.aspx*. These offer you essential, pertinent, expertly researched information on a number of key issues, including Web 2.0 and Green IT.

Training and Consultancy

IT Governance also offers training and consultancy services across the entire spectrum of disciplines in the information governance arena. Details of training courses can be accessed at *www.itgovernance.co.uk/training.aspx* and descriptions of our consultancy services can be found at _www.itgovernance.co.uk/consulting.aspx_. Why not contact us to see how we could help you and your organisation?

Newsletter

IT governance is one of the hottest topics in Business today, not least because it is also the fastest moving, so what better way to keep up than by subscribing to ITG's free monthly newsletter *Sentinel*? It provides monthly updates and resources across the whole spectrum of IT governance subject matter, including risk management, information security, ITIL® and IT service management, project governance, compliance and so much more. Subscribe for your free copy at: _www.itgovernance.co.uk/newsletter.aspx_.

CPSIA information can be obtained at www.ICGtesting.com
Printed in the USA
BVOW011704121011

273475BV00004B/4/P